"I thoroughly enjoyed Dr. Barrett's book and would recommend it to all pastors and anyone interested in kingdom advancement. How encouraging and inspirational are the stories of the pastors and local congregations seeking to find new life as well as transformational hope. I encourage you to read these stories and ask God how he can touch your hearts as we all seek to see congregations revitalized. I appreciate the emphasis on prayer included throughout the book. Thank you, Dr. Barrett, for this encouraging and hopeful book!"

—**RON BLAKE**
District Superintendent, Indianapolis District,
Church of the Nazarene

"A window into the spirit of kingdom building and the kingdom builder. Dr. Desmond Barrett's new book journals the stories of ten congregations, their decline and revitalization in a changing culture, opening a picture of God's continued creative redemptive plan in the body of Christ. Pastors and leaders, this is a must-read in an age of church decline. Dr. Barrett's summary for each congregation opens windows to prayerfully consider as the Lord seeks to renew his church in this day and hour. My heart was encouraged and inspired by these kingdom-building pastors and congregations, the strength of God's calling in very challenging circumstances, and the Holy Spirit's extraordinary intervention."

—**PAUL R. HARTLEY**
District Superintendent, Alaska District,
Church of the Nazarene

"Dr. Barrett is one of the most positive and visionary leaders I know. God has given him the unique ability to see things as possible that others see as unattainable and even hopeless. This short book on revitalizing the declining church will set a confident tone in any leader's heart and give them a can-do spirit, which is an absolute necessity in today's church climate. The words in this book not only come from his sincere heart, but also from his experience, which is rich with both disappointment and great success. I highly recommend this resource and the leadership perspective it provides to the local church."

—BRET LAYTON
District Superintendent, West Virginia South District,
Church of the Nazarene

"We have long needed a practical and insightful resource that provides hope and help for the church's revitalization. Dr. Desmond Barrett has given us that very thing. Read this book if you would love to see the church experience revitalization!"

—TIMOTHY CRUMP
District Superintendent, Southwest Indiana District,
Church of the Nazarene

"Dr. Barrett gives hope and encouragement to the discouraged pastor and struggling church. I wish I had my hands on this work when I started at my first church. It was a struggling and declining church much like described in the pages before you. Dr. Barrett reminds the bride of Christ that it needs to pray and seek God for wisdom through reaching those in the community. This book speaks to the majority of churches today. There is one thing in common: for every turnaround church that prayed and sought God's guidance, the communities were affected for Christ and the church was strengthened again—a true turnaround."

—DOUGLAS S. WYATT
District Superintendent, Eastern Kentucky District,
Church of the Nazarene

"'Can these bones live?' Yes! *Revitalizing the Declining Church: From Death's Door to Community Growth* is an insightful and inspiring read I highly recommend for every pastor and church leader. Dr. Desmond Barrett writes with passion for Christ and from personal pastoral experience as he shares ten relevant revitalization stories of struggle and victory from leaders on the frontlines of ministry. This book is a great reminder that new life is always possible through God's faithfulness and the power of prayer."

—KYLE POOLE
District Superintendent, Georgia District,
Church of the Nazarene

"Dr. Desmond Barrett's book is a must-read for pastors and local churches who have become dissatisfied with the routine and mundane—declining attendances and lack of inspiration and hope, as well as lack of influence in their communities. The ten short stories of revitalization are strong, spiritual proof that God still works in and through faithful pastors and church leaders who are willing to step up instead of shrinking back from their God-called assignment!"

—DANIEL W. COLE
District Superintendent, Nebraska District,
Church of the Nazarene

Revitalizing
the
Declining Church

Revitalizing
the
Declining Church

From Death's Door to Community Growth

Desmond Barrett

Foreword by Harold B. Graves Jr.

WIPF & STOCK · Eugene, Oregon

REVITALIZING THE DECLINING CHURCH
From Death's Door to Community Growth

Wipf & Stock
An Imprint of Wipf and Stock Publishers
199 W. 8th Ave., Suite 3
Eugene, OR 97401

www.wipfandstock.com

PAPERBACK ISBN: 978-1-7252-7951-3
HARDCOVER ISBN: 978-1-7252-7952-0
EBOOK ISBN: 978-1-7252-7953-7

04/05/21

Contents

Foreword

ONE CANNOT OVERESTIMATE THE power of prayer in the renewal and revitalization of a church. The apostle Paul reminds us in Colossians 1:18, he (Christ) is the head of the body, the church; he is the firstborn from among the dead, so that in everything he might have the supremacy. (NIV)

Kyle Bueermann reminds us, "As the head, He alone has the power to bring back to life a church that's on the brink of death. The good news is, of course, that He loves to bring things that were once dead, back to life."[1]

Throughout his book, Dr. Desmond Barrett profiles courageous pastors who are charged with the daunting task of leading churches on the verge of death to new life. While the steps taken toward revitalization are unique to each case study, the one consistent theme repeated in each church is prayer. Revitalization can only take place through a revival of prayer. Prayer revives the people of God, renews their passion for ministry, refocuses on mission, and revitalizes the church. In this book, Dr. Barrett clearly illustrates the power of prayer in the renewal and revitalization of

1. Bueermann, Kyle, "The Power of Prayer in Church Revitalization," *Lifeway Research*, August 30, 2019, https://lifewayresearch.com/2019/08/30/the-power-of-prayer-in-church-revitalization/, para. 5.

the churches he interviews and chronicles. While prayer is not the end all, it is the starting point in each situation. He concludes by encouraging revitalization pastors to pray, go, return, and adapt.

This book will be a source of engagement and encouragement to those pastors who are entrusted with leading a church in need of revitalization. The good news, Christ, the head of the church, loves to bring things that were once dead, back to life.

Dr. Harold B. Graves Jr.
President of Nazarene Bible College

Preface

GOD HAD BEEN TUGGING on my heart for nearly a decade before I fully surrendered to his will to move into ministry in my early thirties. That first summer in ministry was about humbling my flesh, strengthening my faith, and laying the groundwork for my ministerial calling in church revitalization. I still remember the shocking feeling as I jumped out of the moving van and looked out across the street at my new neighbors, a cattle and chicken farm. I was no longer in sunny southwest Florida, but the mountains of rural Appalachia. Moving from a county with over 750,000 residents to one with less than 50,000 challenged me early on to adapt to the new culture God had led me to.

Each Sunday, I would arrive early at the church, stopping at the end of the driveway to remove a piece of board. Reaching my arm into a hole, I would turn on the water from the road to the building. After unlocking the building, I would flip on all the lights, turn on the air conditioning, and stop by the restrooms to turn knobs on the toilets to fill the back tanks with water. There were many times I asked out loud, "What am I doing? From running a multi-million-dollar business before I entered ministry to running a church of eight people with a $20,000-a-year budget."

Preface

There was a piece of me that was depressed, angry, and unsure of why God had placed me at this church.

Sunday after Sunday standing in the tiny foyer before anyone would arrive, I would stare out the double doors towards the church's long driveway crying out in prayer for God to send us a family with children to join the church. Week after week, it seemed no one would come except the same eight members. Was God even listening? Did he even care? The answers would come back "yes" over time. God would send a family and others, but first, he wanted me to die to my desires for ministry to take up his hopes for the church. During these desperate times of prayer, God had laid on my heart a plan, a journey really, a journey of a thousand days to revitalize the local church spiritually and physically. The journey would see us rally to paint all the ceiling tiles in the building ultra-bright white as we did not have enough money to replace them. We would paint the dark wood-paneled walls white, lightening up the dark hallways. A group cleaned out classrooms, sealed the leaking roof, planted flowers, hung banners in the sanctuary, and redecorated the foyer. These changes went over on some like a lead balloon. Even though their discouraging words hurt me personally, God gave me a peace to keep moving forward in his plan.

Over time God would call me to my next ministry assignment where my family and I lived in old Sunday School classrooms, sharing the space with the youth room. While it was not ideal and there were many challenges that I will not detail now, we saw God move compellingly, and it taught me that God shows up in the most unlikely places to do the most extraordinary things. It was through these humbling experiences that I wrote this book. Like you, I have been a pastor of several struggling churches. I have served with people who loved Jesus but did not love each other. I have been cussed out by a board member and left broken-hearted by church members who gave up on God's dream for the local church as they slipped out the side door never to return. I want you to find hope for even the direst situation that a church would face in the pages that follow. You might be under stress and in a challenging assignment, but it is in the struggle that God's spirit is leading. Each chapter speaks about a church like yours. They have church bosses, historians, and pioneers who want to hold on to the past and fight change—the chapters ahead are filled with revitalizers facing crises and overcoming them as they moved from death into community growth. These churches are not mega-churches; they are the average church in America, with an active membership of fewer than a hundred people.

Church leader, this book is for you. It is a compilation of my doctoral dissertation. More than research, it is a window into what other churches your size are facing as they have fought from moving their church from death to revitalization. Be encouraged, pastor—you are not alone. The God who has helped these churches is still helping others. At the end of each chapter, I share five Revitalization Rewards, to sum up how God helped the local church move forward. Ponder each of these rewards. Let them remind you that these are steps and not one magic bullet that turned around a church. All the churches in this book went through a process of decline to a turnaround. For some, it was decades in the making. One thing they had in common was a leader who was willing to do the hard work of taking the first step forward. Sometimes it was one step ahead and two steps back, but the leaders found strength in God's Word to keep stepping forward. May this book encourage you to keep stepping forward to achieve the God plan that he has for your life and the local church.

Serve well!

Dr. Desmond Barrett

1

Shepherdsville

Awakening Hope

Faithful to the Call

THE PASTOR AND HIS family would set up for church in an elementary school gymnasium weekly, and no one came. Nearly a year into the church plant, the pastor grew frustrated as he rolled the piano down the long hallway from the music room toward the gymnasium. In a conversation with the Lord, he asked, "Lord, did I miss you? Because if we do not have anyone this Sunday, then I will close this work believing I had missed you." God would show the pastor that he heard correctly. That day a family with children would peek around the corner and ask if they were in the right place to attend church. For the first time in a year, someone other than the pastoral family would visit the service. It was a reminder that God does not always act when we want him to, but he moves when the timing is right. The pastor had toiled alone for nearly a year, and God would bless his faithfulness throughout his four decades of service to the church.

Over the next eighteen months, the church would begin to grow. Slowly at first, but she would start to run, on average, at least fifty members each Sunday. The pastor realized that it was time to invest in a property of their own. Shepherdsville Church would purchase a small farmhouse and land. The converted farmhouse would enable the church to keep growing and begin to dream bigger dreams during the years ahead. Within the first decade of her birth, the church was averaging fifty-six in weekly attendance with many young families and set her sights on building out the property to reach the community. God had given the pastor a more significant dream to reach the city by adding a Christian school and child care center. "The faithfulness of the pastor and the vision he planted in this place has lasted decades," the revitalizing pastor shared. For forty years, the founding pastor would lead the church to stable and steady growth, leading several building campaigns, building a sanctuary, fellowship hall, and classrooms. They began purchasing homes that bordered the property to convert into child care spaces as the school and daycare were welcomed by the community and were growing at a rapid pace.

God would use the faithfulness of the founding pastor to help transform God's dream into reality. As the church entered her fourth decade of existence, the founding pastor's health began to wane. Members began to ask, what will happen once he passes? They had known no other leader up to that time. They could not dream of another pastor leading them. The pain of his eventual loss would force the church to turn to a new leader. They would push back against any movement of change as they felt bound to what had been done in the past. They were unable to think about a future without the founding pastor leading them.

A Time Capsule to the Past

Three years after the death of the founding pastor, the church still struggled with the legacy that he had left behind. Any suggestion of change was rebuffed by the pastor's widow and key leaders within the church. A small, close-knit group became the keepers of the flame to the past. The more tightly they held onto the past, the more people left, disenchanted by the power struggles forming amongst members. For the "keepers," it seemed no preacher would be "good enough" to take over the founding pastor's mantle. For the ones willing to move on and prepare for the future, they were either silenced by the keepers or left the church. As the keepers hold got more robust, the fellowship got smaller, and they would work to enshrine the legacy of the founding pastor throughout the building. The keepers would place a large portrait and other relics of the founding pastor in the foyer as an imposing reminder for all who walked into her doors that the pastor was as crucial as the Christ they came to serve. For outsiders, the church could seem cold, standoffish, and trapped in a time capsule unable to move forward in new ways but for the keepers it felt safe and comfortable.

The keeper's mentality would result in stunting the church's growth and the original vision to reach the community. The church would stop all outreach programs beyond the daycare on her grounds. The once vibrant church had fallen to just nineteen members on average each Sunday. The Christian school that had been brimming with children was now closed, and the daycare, the only bright spot, took on the burden of carrying the church through cash infusions as the church could no longer independently maintain itself. With $25,000 in debt, the church board did their best to keep her lights on, as they paid interest only on the loan unable to pay the full amount owed each month. As more and more funds were diverted from the daycare to the church, the upkeep on daycare began to wane, and multiple buildings on the property needed remodeling as the years of no investment began to show. The church needed a shepherd to lead her, but were the people willing to follow and adapt to the changes necessary to re-start the church?

Realizing the Need for Revitalization

The eager pastor showed up for his first walk-thru of the property, and he could see instantly the church desperately needed direction. "As I stepped into the sanctuary, it felt gloomy, more like a dungeon than a house of worship to the Lord," the pastor shared years later. The tour would reveal a lack of maintenance, the room's filled floor to ceiling with items, and bleak finances. The pastor would not only have to transform the grieving hearts of those who remained but challenge them with a vision to move forward. The revitalizer would lead with humility, honoring the past and addressing the church's present dismal state. The first month of the revitalizer's tenure was challenging as he moved to avoid the roadblocks placed by the keepers. "There was only one glimmer of hope that things could change, and it came from a group of ladies who prayed on Tuesday nights at the church." From the embers of the prayer meeting, the pastor would fan the flame of prayer, which would spread through the rest of the church. Prayer and fasting would become the catalyst against the darkness of complacency, pushing aside roadblocks, and propelling the church into a new ministry season. If the church was going to embrace a brighter future, the pastor said, "My people had to buy into the prayer times and surrender their will for God's."

The revitalizing pastor would structure every activity and every service around a prayer component. Prayer would not just be a passing fad, or a ritual done as part of the service; prayer would be the heart of the church. "Prayer is the one thing we stand on. It is our foundation for everything we do." The pastor had to reteach the people how to pray. He would walk his people through scriptures, observing Old and New Testament teachings on prayer. He modeled simple structured prayers and encouraged his members to share their prayers out loud with the group. Wednesday nights would become a dedicated prayer night where the church would pray about the needs, desires, and the will of God for a full hour. Shepherdsville was determined to pray heaven down, beating against the gates of hell to save the lost, and to reclaim their community for Jesus. Through prayer, God led the people to see the community around them as their mission field. The city needed spiritual and physical food to strengthen their body. With an enhanced spiritual body (the community) around them, the church body became more potent in sharing the gospel in a new way.

The revitalizing pastor sought opportunities to team up with other ministries, non-profits, and outreach centers. He understood that he did not have the resources of people, finances, or time to start something from scratch. He found several areas open to a partnership through intentional connecting of the dots between the churches and organizations meeting the demand. The pastor began attending city council meetings where he was invited to pray before meetings, attended small group gatherings of other religious leaders from all faiths in the community, and became active in the community by showing up and saying yes when opportunities arose. Through these intentional times, he built personal relationships with key players in the city that enabled the revitalizing pastor to be approached by the region's largest food bank to start a food distribution program through the church. The church prayed and believed that God led them to become the distribution hub that was needed in their portion of the county. The church was not sure how to do it, but they had a willing spirit to try something if it meant God was in it. "God formed it for us. We could not have done what has been done, except through God's plan and our obedience," the revitalizer shared. What once were classrooms filled with things from the past were now cleaned out and replaced with shelving and tables. These rooms would be dedicated to serving others.

Ordinary People Who Believed They Could

Throughout Scripture, God used ordinary people to do extraordinary things. God was taking an average struggling church and was about to open up door after door for the extraordinary. "The people had to catch the vision. It became transferred into their hearts, and they began wanting to do more," the pastor shared with passion. When they prayed, the people saw that when they trusted God for direction and had a willing spirit, God would use them. The distribution pantry would move from a come-and-go pantry to a holistic ministry where people are prayed for, counseled, helped with job prospects, and a resource center for other nonprofits to disseminate information. This was just the beginning of a twenty-four-month period of growth where the church grew out of their comfort zone into the God plan that transformed the church. During this time of growth, the community began to see the church as a community partner rather than a religious center. When students at a local high school could not afford caps and gowns for graduation, the church raised over $6,000 from the community to provide them. When fifty needy families could not provide Christmas to nearly 250 children, the church partnered with another ministry to make sure every child had several toys to open on Christmas day. When families with children were not coming to them, they decided to go to the families. They would form two Parent Affiliated Congregations (PAC) and go into a poverty-stricken apartment complex and mobile-home park to hold church. These targeted children churches would bloom and become a model for other similarly sized churches within their denomination.

Before the revitalizing pastor, Shepherdsville had one child attending; now, they reached nearly 350 monthly through this innovative form of doing church. Over time the small band of mighty church warriors wanted to do more with the children than show up in their neighborhood with the gospel. This would lead them to raise $12,000 from inside the church and community partners to purchase a van to transport children from their area to the church. Through it all, God would bless them with a 25 percent increase in attendance. "I am benefiting from all the hard work that we did together to get where we are today." The pastor shared in numerous conversations that there were so many hard moments where he wanted to give up, but God would not release him from his call at Shepherdsville. The hard work, dedication, time, and effort were now paying dividends as the pastor looked back to those long days and tough nights. For many first time, pastors revitalizing a church sounds easy. Change a few things, paint a couple of walls, and people will come, but the reality is that reviving a church is not easy; in fact, it is very hard. "The smallness of the church does not have to reflect the church's effectiveness in the community," the pastor shared as we sat talking about the nearly five years he has been sowing into this work. "My people realized that God's work is not done in the pew, but through an effective and purpose-filled ministry that impacts the community, one life at a time."

Shepherdsville had awakened to the hope of a better tomorrow by becoming prayerful and faithful to God's will.

What More Lord?

In a year (2020) when many churches lost ground due to a once-in-a-lifetime pandemic, Shepherdsville opened their hearts to expand the kingdom through expanded compassionate ministries programs. The essential connections that they had made in their community and county in the years before would now allow them to expand God's handprint on the hearts of the lost. When elderly residents were trapped in their house and unable to go shopping for fear of catching the COVID-19 virus, the church applied and received a grant which enabled them to purchase a minivan to drive throughout the county dropping off needed food boxes. The pastor, with the approval of the church board, named this new ministry Boxes for the Needy, which started small but has grown to well over fifty families impacted by COVID-19, sustained by the love of a church that has found a new future in connecting with the community. With more and more families using the food pantry due to high unemployment and other virus-related shutdowns, the pressure on the food pantry forced the church to consider pulling back serving others or seeking more help. Again, the connections made over the years helped Shepherdsville reach out to city and county leaders for help. Businesses and city leaders invested over $30,000 into the feeding effort through donations and grants.

A few short years ago, Shepherdsville was on its deathbed, waiting for someone to tell them it was okay to die and close their doors. They had no hope or a vision to go on much further. The leader who had birthed them had gone on to glory. The building, once vibrant and filled with children, had become a tomb of past dreams and hopes of their fellowship. The church went through the motions of doing church week after week, with no outward emotion for serving others outside of their walls. While the people thought God was done with the church, He was about to do something special in their midst. God was sending the right leader at the right time, who would lead them into the next phase of their ministry. The revitalizing pastor took on the challenging call with passion, prayer, and conviction. He led the church to become an outreach post of hope, healing, and help in the community around them. It has not been easy for the revitalizer, and he still pushes up against the keepers who want to hold on to the past, but he won't give up on what God wants to do through Shepherdsville. Remarkably Shepherdsville still has fewer than forty attendees at an average worship service, but impacts hundreds throughout its community. It goes to show that any size church that has a willing heart to reach outside their four walls can impact their community with the gospel physically and spiritually.

Revitalization Rewards Found in the Work at Shepherdsville

1. God does not always act when the church wants him to, but he moves when the timing is right, and the leadership is ready.

2. The leader should always lead like Christ with humility, passion, and promise looking towards the future.

3. Prayer is not a onetime act during a service but a purposeful time of worship in everything.

4. Outreach does not have to be church-led. Find an organization that is doing service well and serve with them.

5. Celebrate the past, stand in the present, but always be outward focused.

2

Grace Community

God Has a Better Plan

Could a New Pastor Help?

As the pastoral candidate was ushered around the property on his first visit of the prospective next assignment, there was no hint of the revival that God was preparing for the people of Grace Community. The church board was interviewing their fourth pastoral candidate in less than a decade, and the weariness showed on their faces. The committee was hoping that a young pastor with a family could help revive the aging church and bring her back to the glory days of the seventies and early eighties. "It was clear that the church had become stuck in a rut. She [the church] looked as if she was stuck in a time warp of the 1970s, with limited updating since that time," the pastor shared. Rooms that had been classrooms of yesteryear had become storage; where children once roamed the hallways, they were now silent, with only a hint of shuffling by the feet of an aging generation. The question the board asked themselves when reviewing resumes was, "Could a younger pastor help us change?" The church knew she was declining and was betting on a young upstart pastor to help restart their spiritual growth. But one question still lingered in the air: "How did a once-thriving family-oriented church become a place where no children played?"

Obedience or Become Obsolete

Grace Community planted in 1964, and was already bursting at her seams by the mid-1970s. Children and families filled her hallways, and it seemed that each inch of the building was used on a given Sunday. By early 1979 the second pastor of the congregation laid out a vision to build a multipurpose building on the property to help with the overcrowding and to prepare the church for future growth. An air of excitement permeated the sanctuary that Sunday, but all were not happy, as some wanted to slow down the changes that had happened with the explosion of growth. Change brings out the real character of those being affected by it. Sometimes for the better, but many times for the worse. The change expands the kingdom, but it pushes against the little fiefdoms those individuals or small groups have built over time as their power base. Within a year, one of the fiefdoms won, and the pastor would leave, and a new pastor would come. The forces that helped delay and deny the last pastor to build the dream God had placed in his heart began working behind the scenes to slow the new pastor. Delay and deny become the determining words in stopping or, at the very least, slowing down the progress for building a new multipurpose complex. Six years would pass, and it would take a leadership change on the board, but the council finally ratified their commitment to the original plan to build a multipurpose building on the property. The victory was short-won. The pastor would leave contemplating what had been missed by not moving forward, frustrated by delay after delay, and ready for a new season of his ministry. Again, the delay and deny group had won out. The third pastor within the decade would arrive, and the delay and deny group would help close the doors of the church.

It was only two years earlier that the church board had reaffirmed the call to build a multipurpose building, but it seemed like decades to those who held on. Instead of following God's plan, the church board deviated and chose instead to buy the adjoining property to the church, which had come up for sale. The church was facing several financial issues at the time. The parsonage needed $21,000 worth of repairs, the sanctuary desperately needed updated carpet, the heating and cooling system of the church was failing, and the board saw the adjoining property as an opportunity to collect rental income. Instead of finding a new revenue source, the purchase stressed an already overstressed budget to near collapse. With the departure from God's plan, it seemed as if God had moved on. Several key leaders in the church moved away because of work-related issues, and families began to leave the church. The church which had been on the cusp of building a new building because of needed space less than two years before was declining numerically and physically at a rapid pace. The onslaught of negative pressures lead the pastor to administer the church with an iron fist, which hampered growth, only escalading the departures of families, and leading to the church to close her doors after twenty-seven years. In less than a decade, the church went from looking to expand to closing her doors because of a lack of attendees. Obedience had become an obstacle to allowing God to move in the church.

If the story of Grace Community ended there, it would be a cautionary tale of a church that was on the cusp of greatness, but experienced failure at every turn because selfish desires kept getting in the way of the Savior's plan. But God was not done with her yet. The church would reopen a year and a half later under the direction of denominational leaders and a church planter to replant the church under a new name while bringing back God's vision to reach the community. The next decade would lead to stable growth and see the church grow to numbers not seen since the heyday of the church. A decade and a half after being replanted, the church was again contemplating expanding her footprint. Yet, discord would lead the church to a painful split as a Sunday School teacher led a spiritual rebellion against the church's leadership. The church would fall from a high of 130 in average worship attendance down to forty, mainly older members, as some took sides, and others fled the division within the church walls. The church was left fractured spiritually, numerically, and financially. The leadership shelved the vision to expand its footprint, as finances became inadequate, and the facility began to fall into disrepair. The church hobbled together the best they could to stay open. Within fourteen months, a sister church was looking to merge after they had sold their property to a developer. With the merger came an infusion of $750,000, which would ease finances, enable the church to fix the items that were in desperate need of repair, and bolster their flagging fellowship. This transition would be the beginning of a new era in the life of the church as three different pastors would lead her in the next six years.

Prayer Would Lead to Renewal

The year 2016 would bring about change, as a new energetic pastor with a family would take the helm of leadership. "The challenge at first was to revise the budget to take an outward posture rather than an inward focus," the pastor shared. Before the new pastor had arrived to begin his assignment, several dozen members filled out a questionnaire that was disseminated during the interview weekend, asking about the church's vision for the community. "It was going to be their ideas and their vision, not mine," the pastor said. The people would power the vision through their ideas, and the pastor would help shepherded them with God's help. Through weekly sermons and monthly meetings, the pastor celebrated the steps the church was taking to reach the community. The celebrations included: Hero Days (lunches for EMS, police, and firefighters), Socks for the Spirit (collecting new socks for homeless families), adopting two classrooms at a local elementary school, and connecting with an immigrant Indian community by providing space to host parties and community gatherings.

Prayer became a significant focus for renewal. In the eyes of some, the people had failed, but the community of believers believed that God would do a new thing. The pastor led the church to refocus on prayer as a tool to prepare them for future service to others.

A church that is going to renew itself for the future and move from decline to growth is a church that needs to have a prayer life that shows it is trusting God with all. The pastor shared that "churches need to pray with a purpose, and I was determined to help lead Grace into a season of godly prayers." The model the pastor used was Big Group—Small Group—Prayer Group, which is done weekly for one hour.

- Big Group—Gather together for a purpose in a dedicated group to cry out to God for direction, vision, and others.

- Small Group—Divide into smaller groups of three to five people to pray over a list of prayer needs (community, denominational leaders, schools, etc.).

- Prayer Group—In the same small group, have members pray for the needs of each member in that group.

Prayer led the community of believers to prepare their hearts for God to use the empty spaces to provide a new home to future community ministries. These connection points would help diversify the church by sharing the property with other ministries as they became three churches at one location, sharing the property with an independent African American church, and birthing a Hispanic church within their walls. The church board and pastor had to balance Grace's needs with two other churches by adapting service times, classroom space, and functionary usage of the facility. The pastor shared that the focus behind these connection points (on/off the campus) was to reach the lost. He stated that they were there to share with the community that the church was alive and active. "The vision was to have the church facility used seven days a week if possible. The community was diverse, but the church was not." Through intentional outreach and opening her campus to other churches in a shared agreement, Grace Community was truly becoming a community of grace. While God used the open campus in new ways, he provided openings in the community to connect to a group that had been left behind by churches. This older population is waiting for a connection with their past selves in senior facilities in the area. During a two-and-a-half-year period, the church would launch seven satellite campuses at area nursing homes to reach new members while expanding the kingdom. For the first time in a decade, the church had moved from decline to growth as they doubled their attendance. Their willingness to be open to God's plans transformed the church into a powerful witness of God's blessing and growing their sphere of influence.

Better Days Ahead

As the church approached its fiftieth anniversary, the board and pastor began to lean into the dream of completing God's plan expanding the footprint of the church on the property. In a deliberate process, the pastor leads the church leadership through multiple steps to agree to design, build, and potentially complete a new multipurpose space that would house their new sanctuary, classrooms, and fellowship hall. Their current space would be converted to a children and youth wing; the offices would stay the same. In contrast, their present sanctuary would keep an eye towards the community as it would become a community space to be rented out, host clubs, and other interest points in a direct correlation to having the community come onto the property. While this was not a new dream, it was a dream that would be challenged, much like in the past. Two current and one former board member, along with their spouses, began lobbying church members to vote against the final building plan. In a small church, it only takes a handful of determined people to derail a dream. These six seemed destined to damage the church as they saw it as a waste of resources and did all they could to discourage the process. "Even as the devil used good people whom I loved to hurt the process, I was determined to see God's plan through, after all, this was God's church" the pastor shared about that painful time.

In the denomination that Grace Community serves, 67 percent of active members have to vote "yes" for a plan of this type to be approved. Two weeks before the vote, the church celebrated its fiftieth anniversary. It was a time of celebration as they looked back and dreamed about the future. With building plans in hand, financing lined up, and forty years of waiting, the final vote was about to take place. "This was a make-or-break moment for the church. Three times before, pastors had led the church to this point only to be rebuffed by a small group of individuals, and they could not get over the finish line to build. If we could not do it, I don't know if it would ever get done," the pastor shared. The day of the vote came, and the pastor sat in his study most of the day praying and seeking God's counsel. The phone would ring two hours before the all-important meeting, and on the other end of the line was a denominational official who had jurisdiction over the church. He was inquiring how the vote would go. The pastor estimated it would be a close vote but was confident they would reach at least the 67 percent threshold needed. It was then the official pulled the vote from happening. "As the snow came down outside my office window, it was as if the heavens were weeping." At the stoppage yet again of the process. "It was the most painful rejection I had ever received in the church. This official had picked the builder, had been part of the design meetings, and had approved the financing options, and now two hours before the vote, he pulled the vote," the pastor shared in a resigned voice even years later. All the work, all the preparation, all the prayers, stopped before a vote could be taken by the people. Once again, God's plan had been stopped. Within two and half months, the pastor would leave the church feeling like a missed opportunity had taken place, discouraged by the lack of forward progress, and disillusioned by the painful stoppage.

With the revitalization pastor leaving, the leadership asked aloud in a board meeting, could an effective revitalization be made in three years? Are three years enough for the people to attain the vision, and was there a willingness to live out the mission once the revitalizing pastor had exited the church? Time would provide answers to those questions. But God was not done yet. God would bring a new younger pastoral couple with children who would pick up where previous pastors had left off. "Coming in, I was impressed with the prayer ministry and their dedication to meeting regularly for prayer. To me, it was of the greatest encouragements and reason for heavily considering Grace." After a year and a half leading the church, the pastor shared several thoughts on the state of the church:

> The church is running strong. Spirits are high; we are making positive, tangible changes to the facilities, and finances will allow us to do just about anything we want to do regarding staffing and outreach. The drawback is that the church will not stay strong for long if we do not close the generational gap—as Grace is heavily geriatric. Our group is receptive to change. They are not very receptive to spending to make those changes happen. I do sometimes wonder if profit trumps the mission in some of our leader's eyes, but they surprised me more than once. They will occasionally approve plans if given solid, researched proposals.

Even in the best cases, revitalizing a declining church is difficult. Grace Community has experienced years of growth, self-destruction, spiritual renewal, God's timing, and historical opportunities. As they move into the future, they are focused on attracting younger families to find a healthier balance of ages and the direction of the church. The pastor stated, "We're heavily considering launching a Parent Affiliated Congregation in-house as a new-start for young families." This could be a key component of their regeneration and continued growth well into the future. In observing Grace Community nearly five years since the first start of renewal, the church has done well to keep moving forward even if it starts and stops along the way. Grace Community began as an aging community of faith, searching for a light at the end of the tunnel after having three pastors in less than six years. They have had a remarkable rebound by opening their doors to two other churches that brought diverse fellowship, solidified through the "togetherness" of three churches sharing a single location. "We can honestly learn much from one another, I believe together we're a solid worshipping body." Six of the seven satellite campuses in senior living facilities are still going strong, with one campus being closed due to a lack of participation, but with the possibility of a new one starting in-house dedicated to young families.

Grace Community is still growing into who God called her to be. She has been revitalized by drawing on a vision that was already inside of the people, as the people just needed to believe that it could be done. In any work of the Lord, there are times of self-doubt, but the Savior has seen this church through some difficult waters, and yet today, they are still developing a community of Grace that will impact their city for decades to come.

Revitalization Rewards Found in the Work at Grace Community

1. A handful of people can delay and deny God's plans for the church.

2. The revitalization leader cannot let discouragement take hold in the people or self.

3. The vision is inside of the people, and the revitalization leader must lead them to attaining the promises inside of them.

4. Develop clear plans with timelines that are agreed upon by all parties.

5. Prayer is the central component to the spiritual and physical change of the church.

3

River City Hope

Revival Culture

Obeying the Holy Spirit

As the pastor walked across the parking lot of the shopping center; he felt a tug by the Holy Spirit to pray for a woman who was just within earshot of him. He began moving towards her with a singular focus to pray for the burden she was carrying, which made him oblivious to what was happening around him. It seemed, the faster he moved, the faster the lady kept moving in the other direction. From a casual walk to a stride, he felt that he needed to break into a sprint to catch her. Out of the corner of his eye, he could see movement but was not concerned about what was happening because he knew he needed to pray with the women who seemed to get farther and farther away. He felt a touch from a strong arm, and he heard the words, sir, you are under arrest, and in what seemed like seconds, he was in handcuffs and pushed to the ground. His mind was racing as one second before he was moving at the Holy Spirit's prompting, and the next minute he was under arrest.

All he could think was; she is getting away, she's getting away, and he began to yell in the direction of where he had last seen the woman, "I need to pray for you. I need to pray for you." It was then he realized his circumstances, that he was the one who needed prayer. The police officer had seen this display of spiritual passion and became concerned that a guy was harassing a lady. After several minutes of uncomfortable conversation as the pastor tried to explain to the officer what had happened, the police officer released the pastor from handcuffs. It was then God used the situation to turn things upside down yet again. This time, the Spirit prompted the pastor to pray for the officer who had just cuffed him. With the Holy Spirit's prompting, the pastor asked the officer; how can I pray for you? The officer began to share how his marriage was on shaky ground, and he was worried he would lose his family. The pastor and the officer bowed their heads, and the spirit of God took over through a prayer. Over the next few weeks, that pastor and the officer would meet several times, as the pastor listened, counseled, and encouraged the officer to help save his marriage. What would have happened if the pastor ignored the prompting of the Holy Spirit? What would have happened if the pastor became timid instead of bold after almost being arrested? One must ask if God was using the context of a lady in need for the restoration of the police officer's marriage. Is the Holy Spirit still working, but pastors are ignoring his prompting?

This story illustrates the revival culture that God has used to revive the pastor of River City Hope and all who attend within her walls. It might seem unorthodox for those unaccustomed to the Holy Spirit's move, but it is a commonplace for those who are members of the revival family called River City Hope. "We are going to break an alabaster jar again and again for the Lord," the pastor shared. The goal was not self-worship but to worship God in everything they do from the moment they walk within her walls of the local church. River City Hope, tucked off a major freeway in one of the largest cities in America, is an urban church in a secular majority city. Viewing the church from the outside, she does not look like a church as it is located in a nondescript strip mall of yesteryear in a rough part of the city, not a place desired by most pastors to house a place of worship. The shops located in the strip mall are sin-filled. From the liquor store addiction poured out; several doors down there was an attorney's office that focused on pedophilia clients; a mob-run money laundering operation was tucked in the corner; prostitutes stood on the corners and walked the parking lot; and across the street stood a strip club. In this strip mall, pouring out with depravities of sin, is where God led the pastor to plant the church to create a revival culture. The rundown strip mall does not look promising to an outsider, but it promised hope for what God was about to do. River City Hope Church is a story of transformation and restoration in and outside the church's four walls. She was birthed with a pastor who was willing to lose it all to follow God's will. It is a place that is decorated with a trendy motif of a hipster church, but its culture is as old as the book of Acts, spirit-filled. Revitalization comes in many forms; it's not only physical, but it is spiritual. River City is a spirit-filled transformative church that is leading others to break free from the bondage that is holding them back to becoming Christ-warriors for the kingdom.

Holy Spirit Takes Over

The revival culture at River City Hope was formed through the pastor's passion for freshly serving the kingdom. A few years before, the pastor was burned out in ministry and was ready to walk away. He struggled in many aspects of his relationship with God and the church and knew he needed a change. Through a spiritual heart transformation, God was going to use him in a new way. God just required the pastor to surrender and surrender he would. As he shared his heart with another pastor in his district, his friend invited him to attend a prayer conference in another state. The pastor thought, "Yeah, just what I need, more prayer." But this prayer conference centered on tearing down strongholds and backfilling the space with God's spirit. For two and a half days, this pastor felt he could not leave. "All I wanted was more Jesus. I did not want to eat or sleep; just wanted more of him," the pastor shared years later. Through this influential prayer conference, God would transform his heart and ministry to come. "If I am honest, I had not ever sought the Lord's presence that way until I went to the conference." The pastor's authentic words are a powerful reminder that people called to serve the church as a shepherd don't always feel the calling after years of pouring out and not getting poured back into. "It was unlike anything I had ever experienced. I knew I was going to give the rest of my life to revival." In a few short days, revival had sprung in the pastor's heart, and he would move any obstacle to conquer evil and shine God's light of love and hope. The Holy Spirit would become his guide.

God Works behind the Scenes

I remember walking into what would become River City Hope Church and thinking, this place is rough and not ready for a church. Over six months, the pastor and a small team of mighty warriors ripped up carpet, tore down walls, and prayed for God's favor to make the place ready for a kingdom beachhead against the darkness that surrounded it. River City Hope was birthed as a church plant of the district to bring light to a darkened part of the city, and God would use her in her infancy to help a dying church rebirth and leave a legacy.

Thirty miles away in the suburbs stood Crestwood Community, a nearly thirty-year-old church gasping her last breaths as she lay dying surrounded by million-dollar homes. Crestwood Community started as a church plant birthed in a local school and housed there for nearly two decades. She would never run more than thirty members on average each Sunday, but she had a desire to reach the community with the gospel of Christ. For many decades she reached families and transplants to the area but could not hold on to large groups outside of their core due to relocations of jobs and families. After nearly two decades of setting up and tearing down, they finally found a piece of property for a long-term home. Unfortunately, the land was tucked away, surrounded by trees and fields. Over time, the community's layout would change as million-dollar homes would surround her, but the heartbeat of new neighbors did not translate to new guests joining the fellowship. "People would have to be looking for the church on purpose to find it," the pastor shared about his time serving two churches at once. Like many churches decades into their existence, Crestwood Community had become a club mentality, where they wanted others to come. Still, they focused on themselves more than connecting outside her walls. Sure, if visitors would wander into the church, they would be warm and inviting, but visitors rarely ever just stopped in.

Crestwood Community would see life change, restoration of relationships, and people come and go as it seemed to attract people for a season. For the last ten years of her life, she struggled to keep a pastor, but a remnant remained faithful to her mission. The church was looking for a pastor, as the last pastor stayed fifty-one weeks, and before that, they went three years without a pastor. The denominational overseer asked if the River City Hope pastor would serve as interim pastor for a short time. As his interim stretched to nearly two years, he felt God calling him to focus on one church rather than two. Unbeknownst to him, God was already moving in the hearts of the remnant that had kept Crestwood Community alive.

After nearly three decades of existence, Crestwood Community voted to close and merge with River City Hope. In a moving conversation with the Crestwood board, the pastor knew God was about to do something new as Crestwood was going back to her roots by joining a church plant to reach the community in need. Though saddened to see the work at Crestwood Community end, the remnant was excited to be a part of something new. "People came looking for something different, but living in a revival atmosphere is challenging because it's uncomfortable, by challenging the status quo of the traditional church," the pastor expressed as he saw some of the Crestwood families leave River City Hope over time. For those that have remained, they have found revival not only in the church body but in their spirits also.

Revival Culture

The culture of River City Hope has been bathed in the foundation and willingness to pray heaven down. Prayer is purposeful and at the forefront of who she is. It goes back nearly a decade when the pastor wanted to walk away from ministry, burned out, and unsure how to proceed. Traveling to the prayer conference radically changed his heart and outlook on the local church. It was no longer good enough to do church; he wanted to experience church. A typical church in most denominations will focus on prayer maybe two or three times during an hour service. Each time it's a short prayer related to something connected to the service, but at River City Hope prayer is the service's main event. Prayer and worship can take up a better part of an hour before preaching is ever begun. The prayers of those gathered can be heard through moaning and crying out to God, with some people on their knees near the stage, others who march around as if on a mini prayer walk speaking to God, still others who stand or sit in silence focused on hearing God in their quite mediation. One would think that as worship would start prayer would end, but it is a continuation of ushering in God's spirit. Prayer is woven into the fabric of worship. Children can be seen waving colorful fabrics of praise during corporate singing, shouts of affirmation fill the air, and words such as "Come on," "Father," "Abba Father," and "So good" can be heard as the worship draws the listener into new intimacy with God.

For an outsider to this prayer culture, it can be an uneasy experience with the Holy Spirit, as the church is non-traditional in her expression of serving the Lord. While the words preached can be heard at many evangelical churches in America, her passion for prayer is unmatched in many regards. It is passionate, committed, prayerful, and worship-filled, all with the sense that River City Hope is sincerely praying heaven down. This revival culture has opened itself to attract broken and hurting pastoral families, some of which have moved across the country to connect with the church, as they come to heal from past hurts inflicted by church members. Other pastoral families come for revival nights held monthly and for times of sitting in the presence of God, soaking in what he has for them. River City Hope's atmosphere is conducive to the healing spirit that has been tarnished by traditional church expectations. The lead pastor has spent many years traveling to struggling churches, pouring into pastors, and their leadership team. He has used his remarkable journey from burned out to sold out as an opportunity to take what he has learned in his spiritual journey to transfer and encourage others in the pit of despair. It's a gifting and responsibility that he has not taken lightly.

The driven revival culture has led the church to launch a twenty-four-hour prayer room online with the focus of bringing intentional times of prayer, worship, and messages into the listener's space anywhere in the world. As they expand their presence online, they are developing an equipping center and school for the practical spirit-filled ministry under their Firebrands Global ministry umbrella. It will give the church a more significant reach to connect with the lost and broken world near and far from their ministry location. As the church continues to find innovative ways to share their passion with Christ, they serve with fewer than sixty people each week as part of their fellowship. God uses their willingness to experience him in a fresh way to see the passion-filled, holiness church connect with a lost community and bring a culture of revival that is transforming everything around them.

Revitalization Rewards Found in the Work at River City Hope

1. A willingness to be used by God in ways never experienced before.

2. Prayer is the singular focus of corporate gatherings.

3. Passion to receive the promises that God has for them.

4. Understanding their limitations and reliance on God for direction, healing, and wholeness.

5. Open to the prompting and movement of the Holy Spirit.

4

New Life

Address Is Not an Accident

Life Support

OUTSIDE THE CHURCH STOOD an imposing "For Sale" sign, a disconnection notice clung to the front door from the gas company, and all the lights were out in the building, or so it seemed. The pastor had arrived for his formal interview to meet his perceptive first church but could not find them. The church sign said she was called New Life, but it seemed there was no life left. Had God called him to bury a church on life support as his first assignment? "It seemed I was being led to a church that was already closed, if not physically, at least spiritually," the pastor shared nearly a decade later. In the early moments of uncertainty, he would search around every corner and open every door to find the people who made up the church. He would find them in a back Sunday School classroom huddled together—fewer than twelve faithful members doing their best to keep the church together. The remnant of believers had sold almost everything to help pay the essential bills, but they were losing their fight to keep the church open. "The members had fought so hard to keep the doors open, yet here they were alone, huddled in a back room." The church was behind on all major bills, denominational budgets had not been paid, and numerically the church had been on a steady decline for nearly a decade. The imposing 20,000-square-foot three-story brick church sat just under a dozen people waiting on God to send his leader to save the church. The leader God had sent them would help transform the hurting church into a heart of service through a missional outlook, but that was yet to be understood by the people huddled waiting that night in the room.

The church had been birthed in 1954 in a once vibrant town. Decades later, the old mill town had lost jobs, income, and people for nearly forty years, and the church was no different. New Life had run out of new life. It seemed guests did not come venturing through her doors to hear the message. The church stood next to a closed mill and abandoned elementary school. The pastor's office was abandoned due to mold from a roof leak, plastic sectioned off portions of the building to keep heat or cold in depending on the season, and as more items were sold off to keep her going, she became more hollow with each passing month. The church had aged, not only physically but spiritually. There was a feeling as if God's presence slipped out of town with the last train that had powered through the city. The question on the lips of those huddled together was, could a new pastoral family help revive this once lively church?

Out of Destruction, Hope

Three times in sixty years, New Life has had to reorganize under the supervision of the district leadership, and two of those times happened in twelve years leading to her renewal. "The church had so many issues, but I trusted God to help lead us to where he wanted us to be," the renewal pastor shared. A year into the pastor's renewal efforts, the church was slowly tackling a host of deferred maintenance issues. "We had a plan, and we were slowly accomplishing much-needed renovations, but resources of people and finances were still scarce," the pastor shared of those early days. As the church inched forward ever so slowly on life support, one night would jolt her back to life with dramatic effect and begin the earnest restoration effort.

A year into the pastor's tenure, two tornadoes hit the county. An EF2 tornado that brought winds of 125 miles per hour clipped the church's side and destroyed homes within a six-block radius. Over fifty buildings were severely damaged, and 267 homes faced some damage. "That night, all we could do was try our best to help. We did not have a lot of resources, but we had prayer and a love for our neighbors to help." The neighborhoods adjacent to the church looked like a war zone. The church itself needed a new roof, but the pastor felt they could do more than pray, they could become the hands and feet of Christ. Out of destruction, the revitalizer felt God instantly give him the vision to reach the city in a new way. Out of tragedy would come triumph. Due to the proximity of the damage, the church campus became a field hospital for supplies, food, and emergency management personnel. For the next six months, the traditional sense of church closed. They stopped meeting on Sundays and, in turn, became a church for the community as they set up a compassionate ministry center serving food, passing out supplies, and providing counseling and rest to the weary neighbors and workers. Day after day, truckloads of provisions would fill the church building and her education wing. An infusion of helping hands and monetary resources came to the church, which enabled her to begin to dream of what God wanted her to do. While the tornado was tragic, God was going to use the pain for a turnaround. New Life was once a forgotten church on the wrong side of the tracks, and in an instant, she became the church of compassion to a hurting city.

With an influx of extra hands, the pastor had groups asking how they could help the local body. Within a few weeks, the pastor began to put into action the plans he felt God laid on his heart during his first month at the church nearly a year before. With the infusion of new resources, a new roof went on the church and education wing. Teams would redesign classrooms; new windows would go in. They added a nursery, built modern bathrooms, developed a food pantry ministry, remodeled a portion of the sanctuary to serve future needs better, and became an active part of the city. The pastor would be given an honorarium from the city commission for his work in leading the effort during the tornado. But with any forward momentum in a revitalization effort, there is always pushback. It would come from well-meaning people who focused on their desires for the church and not God's.

Hide and Seek Jesus

Behind the pulpit was a traditional canvas picture of Jesus that had been given in honor by a prominent family decades before. In every church, there are relics of the past that become saintly, almost godlike, relics. If removed or, in some cases, moved, these relics have split churches, and this picture of Jesus was a relic that would cause trouble for all involved. The revitalization pastor saw the need to add a cross to the platform and removed the picture of Jesus, placing it in a closet for safekeeping until he could find a new suitable location. In its place, he made a wooden cross to be a reminder of what Christ had done for the world. Sunday came, and instead of seeing the wooden cross on the stage as he turned on the lights for Sunday worship, he saw the picture of Jesus looking back at him. "I did not understand the attachment to the picture. Jesus should be in the hearts of the people, not hung on the wall." On Monday morning, Jesus came down, the cross went up, and the pastor tucked Jesus' safety away in another part of the building. Sunday came, and the pastor looked at the platform expecting the cross, but there was Jesus again looking back at him. Monday came, and Jesus came down again, and the cross went up, and this time the pastor hid Jesus in the attic, knowing for sure no one would find him. Come Sunday, the pastor felt confident the cross would be there, but there hung Jesus looking back at him. This story is humorous, but it illustrates the willingness of church members to fight revitalization. Comfort over current needs overtakes serving God to serving self.

A few months later, the pastor would leave the church for a larger one on the district but would share the story about hide-and-seek Jesus with the new pastor as a warning of what was to come. Two years later, the Jesus picture would be moved again, this time in an effort for the second revitalization pastor to redecorate the stage. Knowing the story of hide-and-seek Jesus, he hung Jesus where the counting board used to be in the back of the sanctuary. This time Jesus did not reappear at the front of the church behind the pulpit. "Knowing the dramatic story about the picture, I had spent two years investing in the prominent member's life, by praying with him, sharing meals, and asking his advice along the way. That first Sunday, I knew it would be make or break as I took out a spiritual withdrawal from the years of deposits I had invested in his life." The pastor met the board member outside in the parking lot and explained to him that because of the new worship set, Jesus would be hidden from view. Jesus deserved to be in a place of honor, so he wanted to show the prominent member where he selected Jesus to be displayed. The member walked in and agreed it was an excellent place to hang Jesus. Seven years after the first hide-and-seek Jesus, the picture now hangs on the wall of another church member's home. The work done in church revitalization is sometimes sowing seeds for a future leader to reap the benefits.

47 Cents from God

New Life purchased its current location in 1994. Forty years before, she stood less than one hundred yards away on what is now an empty parking lot. In 1971 she moved to her second location across town, but God had drawn her back to her humble beginnings. During the ensuing decades, the neighborhood had changed, but the church's mission had reverted inward. She had missed several opportunities to connect with her neighbors and needed her passion for the lost back. New Life needed to embrace in a more significant way the mission field right outside her door. After two years, the original revitalizer transitioned out of the church. Denominational officials looked for someone to carry on the work. With the consent of the church board, the next revitalizer was appointed. He would serve for nearly four years, and during that time, God would stretch the church's faith to reach new people with the gospel of Christ.

The pastor was on his third treasurer in three years due to the increasing financial strain that the church was under. God had blessed the church with numerical and spiritual growth, but she sat in an area with 25 percent poverty around her. It was a hardship, but also an opportunity to serve her neighbors in a more meaningful way. As the pastor sat in his office one evening, the treasurer walked into the room, looking distraught. She said; Pastor, you announced today that we are going to start a clothing closet, but we have no money. The pastor asked, "Have all the bills been paid?" The treasurer responded, "Yes." The pastor asked anther question more pointed to her faith: "So, what is the problem?" In a worried voice, the treasurer replied, "We only have 47 cents left in the checking account, and we have no funds in savings." With 47 cents, God was going to do a miracle. Within a few days, a local air conditioning company donated funds for paint and other costs, and a Baptist church in town supplied volunteers to sort and hang five truckloads of clothing.

Within the first year of the ministry, over 1,000 people were helped, and thousands of items were given away. The fellowship hall had sat empty on most days now turned into a hive of activity designed around the idea of a compassion center for the neighborhood. It would host an expanded food pantry, food line, soup kitchen, clothing closet, and teaching space. God used .47 cents to impact the neighborhood in a tangible way. With compassion came the spirit. The pastor took the old pastoral office that once had been abandoned due to mold from a leaky roof and turned it into a dedicated prayer room. Weekly prayer meetings and extraordinary times of called prayer ushered in the spirit of protection as the church fought against demonic forces of poverty and drugs that surrounded the church. Through prayer, God would sustain the mission of the church.

The Mission Challenge

The youth group was meeting upstairs in the church, but downstairs on the edge of the parking lot stood two teens trading drugs for cash. One of the teens came up the back fire escape and entered the youth room. The pastor's wife, who was watching the exchange from the second-floor window, had chosen to either dismiss the young man or invite him in. She decided to invite him. That one act of kindness opened the door for her to invest in his life, which would pave the way for him to come to know the Lord. "My wife and I believed that if we provided a safe place, developed trust over time, that a teen or an adult would be more willing to hear the gospel," the pastor shared. "We opened our home to those in need, and we did it willingly because Christ would do it." The pastoral couple lived inside the church in old Sunday school classrooms as the church could not afford a traditional parsonage, and living in the church enabled the pastoral family to connect to the neighborhood in a unique way. From block parties to youth nights, the church and pastoral home were open to serve others.

In six years, God had taken a church of less than a dozen and grew it to nearly sixty active members. He had used two revitalizers, a tornado, and 47 cents to move the church from the pew into the streets. As the second revitalizer left for another ministry outpost, the church was faced with either progressing or regressing. She has since reverted in several areas, from closing the soup kitchen and clothing closet, while watching the attendance decrease by 50 percent. She has since stabilized, and new life is coming back to her again. As New Life has shown, revitalization is not done or sustained overnight. It is a continual progression of purposeful actions to reach out to the people around the church. As the church prays for God's direction, they are going back to the basics, developing a dedicated prayer night, focused-ministry outreach programs, and intentional discipleship.

Revitalization Rewards Found
in the Work at New Life

1. A willingness to adapt to whatever situation the church faces.

2. A spirit of never give up.

3. Dedicated times of prayer and spiritual focus.

4. The people in the neighborhood were as important as the people inside the church.

5. God can use a mess for a message of hope.

5

Calvary

Fighting to Stay Alive

A Costly Move

THE PASTOR'S OFFICE WAS filled with mementos of decades past. Much like the current state of the church, the office was in a state of change. It was not always this way. Calvary was once a vibrant church of over 140 active members. In 1974 as the neighborhood around the church began to shift, Calvary decided to move further out into the county. They attempted to get away from the changing demographics of the approaching community. Instead of adapting to the changing cultures in the neighborhood, they decided to move. Calvary would essentially become a commuter campus with members driving in three times a week for services, never really becoming a part of the new neighborhood that they had joined. "A lot of the new neighbors were original homeowners in the community. They knew we were here but were not interested in attending the church," the pastor shared in a resigned voice betraying the hurt and struggles of the last fourteen years he has led the church. One community member stated, "I have driven by the church for thirty-five years and hardly noticed it [church] was there." Calvary was built upon a hill, an imposing structure that could be seen by passers-by, yet seemingly missed by the neighborhood. Across the

Revitalizing the Declining Church

street from the church is a thriving child care facility, and it is just off of a major thoroughfare of the city. Calvary should be a church where people flock to and not away from, but for many years pews have sat empty and classrooms dormant of children's laughter.

In evaluating Calvary, it is easy for the reader to reflect on the past mistakes of the church and see the warning signs flashing across the page; relocation of the church due to demographic mistrust built a fortress that kept people out rather than a church inviting them in. Like so many churches before, it is not one decision but multiple decisions that lead a church to the brink of closing. For Calvary, the faithful decision to relocate would sow the seeds of a future failure. Early on, there were warning signs. Within the first three years after relocating, the worship attendance began to wane as members were unwilling to drive out of their neighborhood to the new location less than six miles away. A church that had reported an average of 140 in worship in 1977 would decrease to seventy-eight in average worship attendance just three years later. The move hurt rather than helped the church. Over the next three decades, the slide that had begun in the late 1970s became more pronounced, so that by the time I sat in the pastor's study listening to his heart I understood his words when he said matter-of-factly, "We are dying."

The church that had such hope for a bright future had fallen to fifteen members, with the average member well over the age of sixty-five years old. It was clear to anyone connected to the church; Calvary was inching closer and closer to closure. In the last decade alone income had dropped nearly 40 percent due to the deaths of a handful of faithful members. The deaths caused the pastor and church leadership to rethink many things, including the pastor's compensation. In a heart-wrenching board meeting, the pastor voluntarily surrendered his weekly pay and took on two part-time jobs outside of the church so he could give back to the church through his tithe. This selfless sacrifice was just one of many steps the church took to keep her doors open. It seemed that every board meeting began with the same discussion about "what should we do?" As income dwindled, the board evaluated every line item in the budget to see where costs could be cut. One of the first areas was to stop buying new Sunday School literature, and the lone teacher began recycling past issues instead of ordering new updated material. The upkeep of the property was deferred until more resources were available, which caused part of the building to fall into disrepair. The pastor started contemplating retirement, sensing that maybe new leadership could help the church turnaround.

With colder months coming and knowing that it would bring increased cost related to heating the large sanctuary for fifteen people, the board voted to move services downstairs into the fellowship hall, thus sectioning off the church. All activities would commence in that space to help save finances as they waited on God to provide direction. "As the church aged, the programs [Sunday School and Youth Group] began to wane, and the church began to have a lot of doubt. We did what we could, and we ministered to the people we had each week," the pastor said as he darted his eyes from mine. At that moment, the pain of loss reflected not only his voice but on his face. The sense of failure on his part and God's for not helping the local church was evident.

Finding God's Purpose

What had sustained this small remnant of believers to keep showing up each week? Was it a habit or faith? At their core, the members had a deep-seated belief that God would provide, even if they could not see a way out. Prayer would be the sustaining seed of faith that kept their ideas and vision for Calvary alive. As they sought God in prayer, they began to sense that he had a renewed season for the church to come. Could Calvary, or any church for that matter, maintain faith as they sacrificed so much of what they knew? Was there an ember of hope that could be flamed into a spiritual fire to keep Calvary going for another year? If so, the pastor felt that only prayer would get them from where they were to where they wanted to go. No program or person would lead them

Still Unwrapping God's Plan

Three years since the revitalization effort began, the pastor said, "Death is hard, but not always bad." He has realized that the church had to die of self-desires to achieve the Savior-reality for the church to move forward. He wishes he could say it has been an easy three years, but it did not come without a cost. He faced massive headwinds from long-term members who struggled with letting go. He faced giving up the church parsonage for something new. He had to lead others in saying good-bye to programs and patterns of doing things, all the while giving over to God difficult situations. One challenging situation that almost broke his spirit was a dedicated family of the church seeking to leave. The pastor spoke movingly about one particular family and how active they were in the church, and then one day it all changed as they abruptly left the church and refused to tell him why they were leaving. It was a reminder that renewal was not easy. It became clear that the past would not let go without a fight. Calvary would have to fight through prayer as roadblocks became opportunities to find God's will amid the transformation. Through earnest prayers, God would provide. Prayer was not just another activity during weekly services or even the fallback position of the church when things got tough. To stay in the center of God's will, they dedicated themselves to become fully surrendered to his will through a renewed prayer focus. We learn from Calvary's story that revitalization churches will face roadblocks. How the church reacts to the roadblock will determine the course of their ministry's effectiveness going forward. The choice that Calvary faced was to either adjust their mindset and spiritual makeup or give up and close the doors for good. For Calvary, they had not come this far to give up now.

As Calvary unwrapped what God had for them, they realized that they were in a unique position to become pregnant again, possibly birthing new ministries. I know what you are thinking, pregnant at nearly fifty years old? Yes, they had hoped to birth new churches themselves, but it became clear that God would use their space in the building to bring about something new in their midst. God determined that the church property would become an incubator for growth and spiritual development by opening unused parts of their campus to other ministries. The Calvary church incubator would begin to stretch to reach new communities with the gospel like never before. Calvary had already opened a satellite campus primarily as an outreach to seniors in an area nursing home. They were already hosting an international congregation connected to their denomination. God was leading them to host an independent global church again, this time one not associated with their denomination when the pastor decided to move out of the parsonage, as he prepared for retirement from ministry.

In consultation with denominational officials, the pastor alerted his superiors that he was contemplating retirement. This move began preparing the church body for an uncertain time and an opportunity for the denomination to help transform the property into a new phase of its life. It seemed once again that God would use Calvary's near-death to birth something new as the officials saw the strategic location of the parsonage and the church as an opportunity to birth a Compassionate Ministry Center. The district's Compassionate Ministry Director hoped to start the center in a location twenty-five minutes away. The Calvary property presented it with the best opportunity to hit the ground running. The church parsonage would become the home of the center's director, and the unused space downstairs connected to the fellowship hall would become the hub of the new ministry center. The church incubator birthed out of a necessity to stay alive would provide space to another African congregation. This time, one not connected to the denomination but connected in the sense that they wanted to serve the Lord. From death's doorstep to preparing to host several new ministries, Calvary has adapted to the original calling on her life in her old age. Once she feared she would die, and the property would be sold off to a developer.

Today, she still faces challenges, but she is adapting to the reality that God wants to use her property to expand his kingdom footprint in new ways. Calvary's congregation is still deciding if they should move forward as a church or be absorbed into the new Compassionate Ministry Center. One thing for sure is that Calvary has fought to stay alive. The small congregation sought God, surrendering their will for his, faced many roadblocks, and saw God move as they sought him in prayer. Calvary's legacy is not her death if that comes, but her willingness to adapt and change to what God wanted to do with the property. In her old age, she has helped birth new ministries, new kingdom opportunities, and her legacy of wanting to reach the community is finally being lived out by three churches and a compassionate ministry center that use her property today. Where once pews and rooms sat empty, today they are filled with kingdom ministries that are impacting the community like never before.

Revitalization Rewards Found in the Work at Calvary

1. There is a cost to change. The revitalizer must be willing to embrace and encourage change to move the church forward.

2. The church has to find its purpose amid the problems they face to attain God's promise for the church to grow in the future.

3. Prayer provides clarity of vision and strengthens the lives of those praying.

4. God can use a remnant of believers to accomplish his will for the local community.

5. Be open to adapt and change 'your plan' for God's plan for the local church.

6

Newton Falls

Between the Open Door and the Grave

Grave Hope

As I STOOD ON the cracked sidewalk looking up at the brightly colored red doors that lead to the foyer of the church, I could not help but notice the city cemetery that butted up to the church property. Off in the distance was a granite grave marker with raised letters on it that read, "CHURCH." While the grave marker represented a family name, it was a grave reminder that Newton Falls was a church standing between the open door of revitalization and entering the final stages of death. She had yet to decide which avenue to journey, and in the coming months and years, she would fight to remain alive and overcome self-sabotage, to achieve the future. Like many midwestern small towns, Newton Falls and her people wanted to go back in time to attain what they perceived as the good ol' days. Newton Falls once was a bustling town where her citizens could hear the train whistle bringing freight and people to the area on an hourly basis. The whistles have long stopped blowing, the car plant which had provided high-paying jobs has shuttered, and empty buildings dot the landscape.

In contrast, opium addiction and economic uncertainty have taken their places. People, industry, employment, and family values were replaced by despair and change. Amid the darkness, God has planted a light of hope. In 1952, a small evangelical community church bought the old Catholic Church property in town and would make it their own. Over the ensuing decades, she would ebb and flow with the economic realities in the nation and the rise and fall of the municipality's population, which would shift as industrial plants opened or closed in the community. Newton Falls would strive to maintain a strong presence throughout each season that she faced. As a nominal church of less than seventy-five people, she served her attendees and her surrounding neighbors with the good news of the gospel. Over time, she fought to hold to traditions and would not face the reality of what was happening before her, which was leading to her decline. "It was pretty clear to me when I arrived that if the church did not change and change quickly, we would end up like the cemetery next door, dead," the revitalizing pastor shared. The theme of holding on to the past and not facing realities would be a constant strain and test for the struggling church in the years to come.

God Send the Leader

The church board was faced yet again with reviewing resumes for a future senior pastor. In the last decade, they struggled to hold on to one leader after another. The board had just terminated the relationship with the senior pastor after he had fired the youth pastor. In less than two months, the church was split in half emotionally and physically as member after member left the church never to return. The district leader presented several names as a prospective pastor, and each time the leadership team agreed on one, the candidate would pull out. Finally, on the third try, the board was able to secure an interview with who would become their future revitalization pastor. The church had not changed much in the ensuing decades of ownership from the Catholic Church to the current. She still had wooden pews that resisted updating, a choir loft that was once filled with voices and now of boxes used as storage, and classrooms with memories of decades long past. "The people were stuck in the past, missing out on the fact that they were close to death and on life support at best," the pastor observed when he came to interview at the church. He was told they had close to fifty people. "I found out the numbers were fabricated because of the split, and I had eight people my first Sunday." Even as he felt misled by the leadership, he was determined to pour into the people and begin to pray about God's plans for the property.

He would set out to see if the people wanted to grow or go through the motions of being a church. "It seemed that many of the leaders were more interested in the titles and task than truly doing something to expand the kingdom," the pastor shared with a hint of frustration in his voice. Herein lay the struggles that were to come as he received pushback from the church matriarch, who was the de facto leader of the members. "I felt the matriarch was stuck in the same position on the church board for thirty years, which had created an entitlement mentality and control issues with her." While she felt like she was serving, she became a hindrance to what God was trying to do. While the board had asked for a God-sent leader, they found out they had to also change with God's man.

At the pastor's first board meeting, he began by asking, "What are the church's sacred cow(s)?" The feedback was sharp and direct. The church leadership would support change, but as long as the pastor did not change too much. One instance represents this time. The revitalizing pastor wanted to add removable cushions to the wooden pews. He was proud that they matched the carpet and would help move the church ever so slightly forward. When the church matriarch saw the pews, she breathed hard, snatched up the cushion, threw it under her seat, and sat down on the hard bench in a public display and criticism of the pastor's leadership. While words were not conveyed, the actions sent a clear message to the rest of the church, the change would not stand.

Change with a Price

The revitalization pastor soon realized that he was fighting the flesh of key leaders. He was facing demonic forces who did not want the church to grow, but instead to stay disconnected from the community so she would die. Prayer would become a central focus of the pastor personally and for the church relationally as the church sought to break the bonds of complacency. "If we sought God and fully surrendered to his will for our individual lives and the church's collective body, we would become the church for the community that they needed." For twenty-one days leading up to a week of prayer and praise, the pastor called Newton Falls to read Scripture, seek God's counsel, and pray for discernment. Twenty-one days of focused prayer would prepare the church for the next step God would have for them. At the end of the twenty-one days, the church would gather with other Christian leaders in the community to worship, pray, and hear the word. For several weeks leading up to this prayer gathering a van with multiple stickers such as "666," "Hail to Satan," was parked downtown, and a heaviness seemed to descend on the town. No one seemed to know whose vehicle it was, but they realized it was a tool of Satan to slow the march of God down. Each night during the prayer service, prayers cried out at the altar to beat back the chains of addiction, complacency, and specifically for the dark forces to leave the town. The prayer warriors that joined the church each night seemed to feel more darkness descending as the week went on instead of getting lighter. "We were wondering was God going to move or not," the pastor shared. That final night the van left the town square and has not been seen since, and the heaviness lifted. "For me, that was the beginning of a breakthrough for our community and our church. We still have our struggles, but that night was a reminder to me and others that God hears our prayers and cares about our needs," the pastor expressed.

Transformation was taking place at Newton Falls through the prayers of those who sought him. "God had called me to be here. I did not feel released, and even when I wanted to give up, God would not let me." As prayer became more prominent, the church matriarch would do everything she could to either stop or at least slow down the progress. During a specially called team leadership meeting, a retired pastor was brought in to share from his heart and teach on letting go of the past to prepare for the future. The retired elder had been attending the church off and on for some time. When the matriarch walked into the room for the meeting, she instantly lost control and began to shout and demand that he leave as it was just supposed to be the board. The pastor and all those gathered were shocked at the behavior. As she threw her papers, she wildly flung her arms and spilled the coffee she had placed on the table and then stormed out. What was to be teaching on leadership taught everyone that if they were unwilling to surrender to God's full will, then it was hopeless even to try with some in leadership. "She was part of the team that called me, but she has fought everything I believe God has wanted me to do," the pastor shared one evening over the phone with me. I could hear the hurt in knowing that God had called him in his voice, and he could not get buy-in from one of the prominent members. He would move forward with or without the matriarch on board.

Change or Die

Personalities can stop God's movement and set back a church for years, sometimes decades. The revitalization pastor decided that he would push past his frustration and stand firm in his calling while moving forward with reaching the community. He began by attending city council meetings, listening for opportunities for the church to partner with nonprofit agencies, city staff, and others in the faith community. One of the first projects Newton Falls participated in was baking bread and other baked goods and passing it out to those in need in the city center. A simple step, but an important one to move outside of the four walls of the church. This early step provided an opportunity to teach the congregation about living the word out by being the hands and feet of Christ to those in need. The faith step would lead the church to connect with another nonprofit it met during the giveaway, who was serving those who were facing addiction. The church already knew they could physically help serve the community; now, they were going to join forces with another agency to fight back spiritual emptiness through a critical collaboration to fight addiction. "Little by little, we began to trust each other, and see God move in a special way."

One member of the church had the heart to serve meals, but the church was not equipped to serve warm meals. However, they had extra freezers where they could collect and pass out meals to those in the community. Through the frozen meat pantry, they have been able to connect with new families and have seen the benefit of their outreach efforts as the church has grown from eight to thirty on an average Sunday. "From having no children except mine to seeing twenty-five to thirty children during Vacation Bible School, children attending Sunday school, and church is incredible. God is doing a new thing in our midst," the pastor shared the day I attended a service. In the middle of the service, the side door opened to the sanctuary, and a preteen opened the door and sat down on the front row to hear the sermon. I asked him after the service why he came, and he said, "I love this church. I did not want to miss it." It was exciting to see how God was birthing future leaders to help lead the church forward.

Newton Falls is three years into a long-term revitalization effort. She has weathered some tough years. She has seen pastors come and go, members give up on her, and still others hold tightly to the past fearful of the future. Fewer than one hundred feet separates the church's front door from the graveyard next door—one hundred feet between the open door and the grave. In the past twenty-four months, the church prepared for guests by redesigning their stage and updated lighting. They have gone room by room cleaning to provide space for the children that have been attending, painted several badly needed areas, replaced old signage to enable visitors to know where things are in the facility, updated their sound system, and participated in community events. Through it all, members and the pastor have had to fight through the discouraging remarks of the matriarch. They have not lost sight of what God has been doing inside her walls. The pastor understands the work has just begun. "While we have accomplished a lot, still so much more has to be done if we are to remain vital in the community." While the pastor's words are of caution, they also celebrate the achievements that he and the leadership have accomplished. The church had several decades of decline and gains and then settled with eight members when the revitalizer arrived. Newton Falls has faced a church split, firing of a pastor, and personal agendas, but God has kept them alive. Why? That is a question that only God knows. All the members know for sure is that God is not done with them yet.

Revitalization Rewards Found in the Work at Newton Falls

1. Letting go and letting God is more important than having a plan from God.

2. Prayer positions people to propel forward to achieve God's plans.

3. Members may self-sabotage, but the Savior can conquer sabotage through fully surrendered leadership.

4. If God has called you, then stay even when it gets hard.

5. Revitalization is not a quick fix; it is a long-term investment.

7

Whitesburg

Holding on for Jesus

The Call

As I WALKED INTO the country church just off a county road in the Appalachian Mountains, I was greeted by a member who shared, "We are holding on for Jesus." I was taken aback as I assumed Jesus was already there in their midst, but I quickly understood it was an expression of her faith, but also firm resilience. Once a thriving coal region, Whitesburg had been hit hard by environmental regulations and shifting consumer demand. Whitesburg was once a town of 2,800 surrounded by valleys filled with families earning top dollar from the coal industry and related jobs. Today Whitesburg struggles with a 23 percent poverty rate, with nearly 30 percent of her children living in poverty. Four coal companies still operate in the region, but they are struggling to ward off bankruptcy and hold less promise for the region's future. A decade before the Whitesburg church founding in 1978, President Lyndon B. Johnson would come to the area as part of his tour on the War on Poverty. Over fifty years later, the effects of poverty are still profound, and Whitesburg has found herself holding on for Jesus to help turn this small church into a thriving church again. The revitalization pastor found himself wondering what God would do through him to help lead the church when he drove into town for his first sermon and pulled into the gravel lot and peered at the white cinderblock square church. Whitesburg had been without a pastor for a year and a half. During that time, she had many rotating pastors who filled her pulpit each Sunday. The people seemed pleased that she was still open and did not mind having a rotating pastor. If life had taught them anything, it was that they could overcome any adversity and hardship.

A few weeks before his first Sunday, the revitalization pastor met with the district leader for lunch. During the meeting, it was clear the church had to change, or the district leader would take Whitesburg off life support, sell off her assets, and reinvest the funds into a new start congregation. "From the conversation I had, it was clear to me; this would be Whitesburg's last chance for a turnaround or death would come." The pioneer spirit of fewer than forty years before had gone by the wayside. The people had lost hope in a full turnaround, but they hoped the church would not close while they were still alive. "Many of the members are well into their seventies and eighties, and it is the church they raised their family in, where they grew more rooted in their faith, and where they found stability as the community changed. The fifteen pioneers who founded the church in 1978 would help it grow through the attractional model. By the mid-80s Whitesburg would peak at sixty-four active members. The decline can be traced to 1988 when a fire that swept through the church's rented property and destroyed all they had. For several years leading up to the devastating fire, the church and the landlord had disagreed over what the church was doing. On several occasions, the landlord tried to pressure the church to break its lease and leave. They felt God had called them to this space, and they were going to honor the contract. A fire would force them to relocate and find a new home to worship in. Several in the church still harbored doubts that the fire was not self-made and not an accident as local authorities ruled it. That suspicious nature sowed itself into the church's fabric and steeled the members to keep the doors open at all costs.

With the devastating fire in the rearview mirror, they chose to relocate to the outskirts of town to a nondescript block building off a county road. A church member would find a hymnal that was scorched but not entirely burned in the burnt shell of the old church and see it as a sign from God. A page from the hymnal would be framed and placed in the new sanctuary. The hymnal was a reminder that the church had come through the fire but had come out with God, and nothing would stop them from being the church that the community needed. As the economic realities hit Appalachia, Whitesburg would steadily decrease to where she was that first Sunday when the pastor arrived, eight people counting the pastor and his wife. "We had prayed about the appointment to Whitesburg and my wife and I felt God's leading to this challenging ministry." The challenge ahead for the pastoral family was to harness the past, deal with present-day realities, and help the church begin to dream again. If Jesus was missing, then he was going to do his best to bring those people back to God.

The Reality

As the pastor and his wife drove around the community, they could see a rich legacy of the past and the present reality that many shops were empty, and homes were boarded up with overgrown yards where families seemed to have abandoned or lost their homes. The opportunities that once kept residents in this close-knit community had disappeared like night turning into day. Whitesburg would be hard soil for any pastor to sow into, but it would be even more challenging for a first-time pastor. "Bible College had prepared me for the theological aspect of leading a church, but only going through a challenge can prepare you for what I faced early on." God had called a middle-aged couple with years of a local church ministry experience, but no senior pastoral experience to help lead a revival and transform God's church. "We knew it would be hard, but I do not think we realized how hard it would be," the pastor shared over lunch two and half years into the revitalization effort. The church sat on the edge of a winding creek, and passersby could have mistaken that she was closed. Bushes were overgrown, weeds protruded out from the flowerbed, vines covered the church sign as they snaked up the wall, and a large cross laid on the gravel parking lot tucked under one of the overgrown bushes, as paint peeled off the walls revealing several shades of color. "I had hoped that someone cared about the church, but from the looks of the grounds, we wondered, would we find anyone inside?" As the pastoral couple stepped foot into the foyer, there was an unmistakable smell of mold that permeated the welcoming air. The entrance could not have been more than three feet wide and eight feet long, sandwiched between the only bathroom in the facility and a stairwell that led to the fellowship hall and classroom space downstairs. The carpet was stained in several places, wrinkled, and drawn up in still other areas. The sanctuary had mismatched pictures hung haphazardly on the walls with two air conditioning units poking out from the platform—one worked, one did not. Dead insects lay in the sanctuary windows, and Bibles were strewn about the pews, with several marking the spot of the church member who would come each week and take their same place. As the pastor went down the dark stairwell to the fellowship hall and classroom space, he would find the mold's location. In each of the three adjoining classrooms, there was mold from the knee down. Two-thirds of each classroom was taken over by things collected and then piled on top of each other. The fellowship hall was aglow with fluorescent lights as the windows had been boarded up and painted over. In the middle of the fellowship hall, three long tables, one for the pastors' desk, and the other two for fellowship dinners finished off the area. What should have been a welcoming area for gatherings was, in turn, a dark and unhealthy space.

Upstairs the eight members of the church greeted the new pastoral couple with warm smiles and hugs. The pastor sensed instantly, "These were the friendliest church people I had ever been greeted by." The members ranged from fifty years old to mid-eighties, with the majority over the age of seventy. The members who were gathered showed their age, as they had once been part of the young families that filled the church decades before. Now, however, the church seemed tired and worn down from days gone by. After his first Sunday, the pastor would turn his attention to understanding the church's financial picture and realizing the church was struggling in several areas. The church had cobbled together a small amount of savings, but within a few months, the church would run out of money. Most of the church's income did not come from the weekly tithes but through the parsonage rented to a family who did not attend the church. The meager rental income of $400 a month helped to pay the church's utility bills and a small stipend for the pastor. The pastor would begin to work for free within his first year as the church could not afford to pay the bills and pay the pastor.

Developing a Plan Forward

"Do you support the revitalization of the church?" that pastor asked the congregation assembled for a special meeting. Those gathered that Sunday answered in the affirmative, yes. In the ensuing months, the pastor would walk the church property inside and out, praying over what God wanted him to do with the church. "The focus was always about renewing God's church for God's people. The calling was never about my abilities or dreams, but the people's." The pastor's style was to work within the confines of the congregation to develop a strategic plan that would effectively reach outside the walls of the church into the community and capture the church's past glory by upgrading the facility to prepare for future guests. He realized early on that the decline in the church did not happen overnight but over two decades, and he could not shift the culture or the decline without first stabilizing the spiritual health of the church. The revitalizer would slowly move in the direction of leading the congregation to change. Developing a long tenure and deepening relationships would become his focus. "When you have a few people and even fewer workers because of age, all you have is time." Time would either lead the church to renewal or closure.

With the help of an outside mentor, the pastor was able to evaluate the property. The pastor and mentor developed ten recommendations for the outside of the church building and twenty-one recommendations for the building's interior. They were as simple as trimming the bushes or removing carpet in the stairwell, but all early recommendations focused on first impressions and preparing for future guests. The board, however, seemed reluctant to move forward on the action steps of the revitalization effort. They had voiced support up to this point but began pushing back on starting the task and working through the recommendations. Some were afraid of change; for others, they struggled with the faith aspect of the endeavor, and still others were stuck on the cost of the revitalization effort. The church was already struggling financially. Less than $1,000 a month was coming into the church through tithes and offering, with most of the funds coming from the parsonage rental. With the pastor and denominational budgets not being paid, could the church afford to invest in itself for a future that seemed so uncertain? "We had to try something on this list, or we were going to die," the pastor shared. He would lead the people through times of focused prayer, preach messages on faith, and listen to the concerns of the members while prodding them forward.

Expecting Jesus

The first-impression list was daunting at first glance, but as the pastor encouraged the board to break down each project into bite-sized chunks, they began to see that progress could be made and that they could prepare for guests while restoring the church. One of the board members' husbands, who was not a member, volunteered to have the outside of the church pressure-washed and painted at his expense, the bushes cut, and the cross rehung on the building. The parsonage renters agreed to fill in the ruts in the parking lot with fresh gravel as they shared the lot for parking, and several members said they would pull weeds and plant new flowers in the flower bed. What looked like a lot of money turned out to be the first of many reminders that God would bless his people's efforts through willing hands.

As Halloween approached, the revitalizer saw it as a perfect opportunity to let the community know that the church was alive and well. He and his wife distributed to nearly seventy-five homes flyers inviting families to a trunk-or-treat that would be held in the church's parking lot. The truck-or-treat would be Whitesburg's first outreach event in a decade. Close to one hundred children and their families came to this free community event. Members were able to invite their neighbors to the church and express their appreciation for the community coming to the church's property. "I had hoped that we would get a lot of families from that event. But not one family came back." While the pastor was disappointed, he would later realize that the church could not expect one event in ten years to turn around their fortunes. It would take deliberate action over time to alert the community that they were welcomed on the property and could join them for services.

After this event, the pastor felt led to make it easier for the community to attend a service by streaming Whitesburg's services online. Utilizing a streaming tool to connect with the community, they began hearing positive feedback from those tuning in. A church that had disconnected from the outside world started to chart a new course. The goal of becoming a welcoming church was getting closer. Through these efforts, the church would see two new members come into the fellowship, and several of the ladies attended a women's retreat to restart their faith in themselves and God. The pastor developed a Sunday night Bible study wrapped around prayer and looking at overcoming adversity. "I realized that we could not give up. God has not given up on us, and we have to keep moving forward." The pastor's faith and the determination of this mighty small band of faithful members have moved Whitesburg closer to renewal than death. However, the seeds of decline sowed for two decades, failure to maintain the facility, and an aging population puts them at risk for closing. With God, they will keep breaking down strongholds and connecting with the community in new ways to keep growing forward. The story of

Whitesburg's renewal still has not been written. What I know for sure is that they will not give up without a fight.

Revitalization Rewards Found in the Work at Whitesburg

1. Determination to keep going is a key element in doing whatever it takes to stay open.

2. Prayer prepared the ground to be mined for faith.

3. One outreach ministry will not turn around decades of decline.

4. There is a solution to every problem if you look closely enough.

5. Revitalization takes tenacity, and a willing spirit to be moved by God.

8

Westwood

Small Changes, Big Difference

Upsetting the Spiritual Apple Cart

"PASTOR, TELL ME ABOUT all the changes," Mary asked as she sat waiting for the pastor to speak. A few days before, Mary, the longest attending member at Westwood, had a disturbing telephone call from her sister, decrying all the changes that had recently taken place in the church. While Mary's sister no longer attended the church, she had watched the latest service on social media and was destressed by what she saw. The pastor patiently explained each move and why it was established as Mary sat silently, taking it all in. When the pastor finished, she asked him to walk with her around the sanctuary to tell her what she was seeing before her. Mary could not see the changes that had been recently made, but Mary had etched in her mind's eye the way the church used to look when she was a little girl growing up in the church. While Mary had slowly lost her eyesight, her heart for Jesus had only grown more robust, and she wanted to understand what had taken place as she loved the church, but Jesus more.

Mary thanked the pastor for being so patient with her as he escorted her to the piano, where she still played several songs each Sunday after the impromptu tour. As she finished her last selection that Sunday, she asked if she could speak. The small gathered crowd leaned forward in their seats and listened as she rose and pushed back the bench that she had been sitting on. She shared that her dad, a former pastor of the church, was a man of change and would be thrilled with all the changes. With that one declaration, she gave her seal of approval to the revitalization strategy taking place on the campus of Westwood Church. The "Yellow Church," as it is affectionally called in the community of less than 5,000, sits on the main street, just a block from the small-town high school and school district administration building. Sandwiched between a Boys and Girls Club, cemetery, a mix of weathered homes, and an abandoned store, the Westwood Church has been in this prime location since 1968. While the church building was built in 1956 and had another life before Westwood was birthed, the church had been a healthy community family church for more than two decades. During her third decade, she began to falter as the young families began aging and moving away, leaving an elderly population. Each Sunday, members of the church would unlock her doors and prepare for guests. In a way, the church members said, "We are here, come and see," yet no one visited. By 2018 the church had been in decline for the last decade and was in a maintenance mode doing her best to keep her doors open for all intended purposes. The district official overseeing the church reviewed the numerical and community decline and counseled the church to either take significant steps in the area of church revitalization or he would have to close their doors. While the official had given options, it was apparent to all those who gathered that declining further was no longer an option. Hard choices would have to be made, which meant giving up what they knew for the unknown.

Westwood would either live or die, but it would be the member's choice. After much prayer, the remaining members who were less than thirty years old voted unanimously to keep their doors open and seek a revitalization pastor. "My thought process was that change had to come. We expected the people to be more open when it did come," one of the co-pastors lamented later. With the last baptism taken place in 1998, two decades before, it was not going to be a smooth turnaround, but the members were saying all the right things until the change started.

Unbeknownst to the Westwood Church, a pastoral couple in another state sought God's direction for their next ministry assignment. God was preparing hearts in two different states to come together as one. In taking the assignment, the husband and wife co-pastor team (referred for the rest of the chapter as "pastor"), would arrive from a northern state into rural southern culture and were initially challenged by the cultural differences they faced. "Coming to a rural region, trying to integrate into a family-dominate culture was hard. On top of it all, outsiders were trying to change everything they knew," the pastor shared. The pastoral team was counseled by the district leadership to go slow in the initial process of becoming Westwood's pastor. "We were told that in revitalization, we needed to have patience and limit changing things quickly. We focused on loving the people. Learning their story and in what the community wanted from the church," the pastor shared. The couple would find a church that was broken, not only spiritually, but physically, by the lack of attentiveness of previous pastors and community disengagement by her members.

So Much to Do

What does not need changing; was the question the pastor asked after the first week. The pastor was seeing the church with a fresh perspective and in doing so could see how uninviting the church was from the street view. The basketball goal in the parking lot was constantly knocked over, letters on the church sign would be changed by passersby or knocked off, and the chipped paint and worn parking lot made the building look old and warn down. "It (the church campus) was not inviting. If I were just passing by looking for a church, I would not feel comfortable wanting to go there,' the pastor shared of that early experience. As the parsonage was only several houses down the street from the church the pastor began trying to connect with the neighbors. It became apparent rather quickly that former pastoral families had done some real damage to their neighbors and it would take more than a coat of paint to change perceptions. In realizing the past hurts, the pastor set out to develop a vision to restructure the church from a 1980s motif to being culturally relevant with the community around the church. The goal was twofold, not to change things to change things, but to prepare for the guests to come, and if by chance a former member would come back, the member would see things were different. "We did not want anything to bring back bad memories, and we tried to replace things with that in mind." As the pastor processed the needs from their vision restructure outline that the board had approved, the pastor found the top priority to change was the music. The pastor had waited six months before a change was made in the church, but the situation was too critical to keep waiting any longer. For any guests who attended the service they would notice that the church sound was stuck in a time warp and for the pastor something had to change and had to change fast. The pastor would respect the past but intended to bridge the divide by bringing the music forward to a more contemporary style. By bridging the two genres of music the church would start off each service with one older hymn and then move into several modern songs and then close with a piano player playing a hymn of yesteryear. "It has been pretty difficult for me as I have lead worship before and now to say let's adapt it this way has not been easy." For any pastor who has experienced the worship wars of the last several decades, the reader knows how challenging this one hot button issue can be. Many pastors have lost their ministry trying to traverse the music culture of a church, but for the revitalizer this would be the first of many difficult decisions made.

As the pastor began the revitalization process, negative pushback become more apparent. Most of the time it was passive aggressive, but it came to hurt personally. Members started leaving, and others began withholding their tithes as a silent form of protest. Members of the pastoral support team began getting worried that this would defeat this dynamic couple. "We know our God is able and will provide," they replied. The faith of the pastor was sustained through dark days as the pushback became reticent.

Where once thirty sat, the church dwindled to under fifteen. As the emptiness of the facility set in, it became clear to the remaining members that the largest tither and a long-time attending family in the church was unhappy. The pastor poured into this family and tried to develop a strong relationship with the couple. "We made an intentional effort to invest in them. They were a long-term family in our body, and we knew change would be hard." As a family unit the family became fractured over the changes that were happening around them in the church. This fracture in the family reverberated in the church with the father and mother leaving the church with a grown child and her family while another grown child and her family decided to stay. While it was heartbreaking and challenging for all involved, God was shifting the culture in the church for the better. The pastor realized that sometimes you have to lose what is comfortable to gain what is God.

Good-bye to the Jesus We Wanted

As the church continued to transform into the church that Christ wanted her to be, the pastor began to move aggressively to change the church culture. "We were going to rip off the band-aid and go all in." The all-in meant nothing was sacred. If it did not move the gospel story forward to reach the community around the church, then it was discarded. In the sanctuary, as in many older churches, there is a scene of Jesus baptism. The pastor wanted to transform the inside of the church radically, and it was decided that the sanctuary would shift ninety degrees. Where once the platform and the baptismal stood, a coffee house would brew in that place. The majestic scene of Jesus being baptized would be painted over with black chalk paint, lights would be strung, and wooden barrels rolled into place, becoming high-top tables. The members had to say good-bye to the Jesus they wanted for the Jesus they needed to reach their neighbors. Where bare white walls stood starkly for decades, a rich hippopotamus gray would take its place; the bright crimson carpet would be rolled up, exposing the hardwood flooring underneath, which was stained a rich chocolate brown. The new platform would be built out of wood and metal sheeting. Flatscreen televisions would replace the old projection system, and chairs would replace the hard-wooden pews. "It was a radical departure of what they had, but it was positioning us for the future," the pastor shared as he pointed out the changes in our walkthrough.

The change continued downstairs as a new children's check-in system would take the place of an open-door policy of the past. While Westwood had fewer than three children, the pastor was praying and preparing for the children and families to come. The space underneath the sanctuary was dark with low ceilings, limited lighting, and small windows that brought in natural light. The halls felt more like a tunnel than a welcoming area for children to learn about Jesus. The pastor began working in one classroom after another turning storage space back into classroom space. Walls were painted with warm natural colors and filled with child-friendly items that brought a comfy-cozy warmth to each classroom. The children's church area transformed from what was a mini-sanctuary with wooden pews and a mini-pulpit to a kid-friendly environment that had a camping theme. Each classroom was redone through the lens of a child and not an adult who designed it.

As each change was made, the stalwarts in the church pushed back as they felt the changes taking place were taking away their heritage and giving the church over to families who would come. This led to more people leaving the church. On the heels of more departures, Westwood's treasurer finally could not take the spending and change any longer. She announced publicly that she had resigned after serving in the role for well over ten years, and she added that she was considering leaving the church. While a mission team from another state helped with many changes, she still felt the church should not spend limited resources like they were doing on a pipe dream of the pastor. This clash of differences has been seen throughout the revitalization process. The "us" versus "the future" battle is still being waged, sometimes publicly and many times privately.

The Work Continues

Two years into the turnaround at Westwood, the pastoral couple can see how far they have come. It has been and still is a challenging assignment. The church has been forced to adapt or die. Westwood chose unanimously early on to live, but they could not die to self-desires and some left the church. "It's been a hard last year. Lots of tears, and lots of doubt, but I am going to keep walking," the pastor expressed with a slight hint of the wounds encountered. Those who stayed have been challenged to let go and allow God to move. Remaining members have adapted with a heart geared toward honoring God. While not all changes have been to everyone's liking, the remaining members have begun to pray for the pastor and are doing their best to support the call to change. Westwood has shown that change is not easy, and the Westwood Church has experienced the pain while receiving the promise that change brings. As the pastor shared, "We still trust God. We have a feeling of peace, and we will not give up on what God wants from the church." The pastoral couple did not come to bring change; they were tasked with change. They were called by Westwood to bring change, and the lack of change over the last decade almost closed the church, yet the difference that change brought has fractured families and decreased the church.

God has challenged the status-quo of the past. The calling was to go into the mission field to replant the area for a future harvest. "Let us shake it up. Let us invite people in. Let us change the culture from what church has been and what people know the church to be," the pastor implored. In this quote, the passion, the calling, and the obedience of this couple shines through. Will Westwood grow and thrive? Will Westwood burn out the pastoral couple? Will Westwood be closed and then replanted? I know for sure that God has been transforming this dying church into a community church by encouraging believers to connect with their neighbors. The church is awakening to God's call, and as the pastor hopes, may Westwood follow through and be the church God has planted her to be.

Revitalization Rewards Found
in the Work at Westwood

1. Have patience amid church revitalization.

2. Limit change until you have buy-in from a portion of your leadership.

3. Evaluate the church's needs with guests in mind.

4. Radical transformation can lead to transformed hearts.

5. If God has called you to a revitalization assignment, he will provide the tools to complete it.

9

Seashore Community
Restoration by the Sea

Stormy Relationships

THE WIND-SWEPT COMMUNITY CHURCH nestled by the sea has weathered many storms throughout her life—none more critical than rebounding from the death spiral. Seashore Community was a steadily growing church that grew to over three hundred over three decades, but by the time the revitalization pastor arrived, the church had fallen to ninety-two members. The church, torn by strife, misdeeds, and misguided leadership, struggled to rebound after a tumultuous fifteen-month pastoral assignment that almost forced the church to close. With the district's leadership intervention, the church was led by an interim pastor for one year. The interim would become the district's eyes and ears and evaluate in real-time the reasons the church was spiraling out of control.

When the revitalizing pastor moved into the parsonage, he would find the remaining members skeptical of each other and questioning the way forward. "I just wanted to love on people. I sensed they were hurt, and I wanted to provide healing," he said as he shared his first impressions. As he navigated those early days, he set about listening to everyone he came into contact with; sometimes, these conversations left him hope-filled, but many times the conversations left him unsure of the way forward. In these "un-sure" times, he would wander down to the seashore and seek the counsel of God in the sounds of the ocean's roar and the rustling of the wind. Throughout his tenure as a pastor, he has found a ministry in the hurting. At Seashore Community, he would help the church through the pain of the past and heal from hurt to attain her future. "Believe in people who you are chosen to lead. Do not worry about their motives when God is dealing with their heart." His humble spirit and love of others would serve the church well as they moved from the courtship to the honeymoon phase and into the hard work of digging up old bones to rebury them properly.

In many ways, revitalizers are archaeologists who examine the past by exhuming where the church has been. While this is a painful part of a revitalizer's work, it helps move the church forward to learn from the past. With past experiences guiding the process, the revitalizer set about exhuming the past, listening to those still within the church. By listening in on one-on-one conversations, small groups, and intentional conversations over meals, he heard four areas of past or current storms that needed to be re-exhumed and addressed before the church could fully move on.

- Lack of communication from the leadership to the laypeople of the church.

- Failed pastoral/church relationships that lead to decline.

- A church-run learning center closed and there was a possibility of it reopening under the right leadership.

- Compassionate ministry center that had a polarizing leader as its head.

The pastor listened to each side, leaned into the conflict, learned from each conversation, and took lessons from what he had learned to move the conversation forward to healing. His spirit of love for everyone in and out of the church kept the church from declining further in those early days of his ministry.

Exhuming the Past

Communication was lacking during the fifteen-month death spiral that saw most church attendees leave with the average worship attendance cut in half during this brief time window. As the revitalizing pastor listened more than talked in those early months, he found members who had different perceptions of what had taken place. The primary complaint was that the average member did not know why decisions were made. Besides the weekly bulletin, the only other way members found out anything was through the church's grapevine. The grapevine soured members with misinformation and innuendos. "When you get tired of saying it, the members are just starting to hear it," the pastor expressed years later. "Say it. Say it again. Keep saying it," has become a mantra of his time at Seashore. The pastor wants everyone to feel they are a part of the decision-making or hear of the leadership's decisions directly from him. Communication is a significant component of a turnaround for any church, and in a revitalizing effort, it can become a component of keeping things moving forward.

Through these interactions, the revitalization pastor laid the groundwork to bring about healing from the tremulous fifteen-month pastorate that had preceded him. He understood he could not lead the people through healing until they knew how much he cared for them. "My first year was about showing up at life events of the members, sharing life with others by being a part of what mattered to them, and being very visible to those who felt invisible during the previous pastorate." The summation of what he had spent months listening to in those early days was the people wanted a shepherd more than a pastor. They wanted someone who cared about them and the issues they were facing, and they found that in a shepherd who loved dearly his flock. As the church shifted into a conversation mentality instead of confrontation, the revitalizer began reevaluating the leadership around him. As some leadership members moved away from the church during the first year due to a host of circumstances, not the least change itself, the change enabled the revitalizer to realign the leadership team to take on the vision of church revitalization earnestly. In doing so, the board became more diverse in mindset and outlook, which lead to a healthy transformation of the church over time. "Today, the church is the healthiest it has ever been. This is the healthiest church I have ever served," the pastor shared after two years. Two years before, he walked into a church that was struggling to maintain members, and, today, she is the healthiest church the pastor has ever served. So, what was the significant change?

In evaluating the church, the significant change was a willingness to exhume the past and not cover over past hurts and pains. This is not for the faint of heart, but it is needed if new growth will be able to grow in an area that once was toxic. The revitalizer understood that by exhuming the past, he might be removing one situation for his own challenges, because the past typically brings up buried hurts. Still, he was willing to be invested long term and to take the short-term hits. His healthy mindset enabled him to address the past in a forward motion that provided a clean space to rebuild on.

Right People in the Right Place

For many, the ensuing years saw two groups of people, the faithful who served as the hands and feet of Christ, and the traditionalist, that came because it was what they always did. In evaluating his leadership team, the revitalizer wanted to give space and permission to those serving out of duty to know it was okay to step aside by celebrating their efforts and sharing with others all their work. This provided the dutybound servants an honorable way out while knowing they had accomplished their God-given mission. The second step was to find potential lay leaders who had bought into the church's mission and vision while having the heart to serve God in whatever capacity he might be calling them. The revitalizer shared, "My heart was wanting to have the right people in the right place to take the next God step in the life of the church." He would not rush this process. Even if a leadership member resigned their position, he was diligent in refilling the position once he had God's assurance. While this did create issues, he understood that this would be a long-term turnaround, not a quick fix, and was willing to take on the extra added burden for a short season. In waiting on God, the church has seen a real transformation of hearts. In fewer than two years, seven people have been called to ministry and are pursuing the path toward ordination. The church board has become more diverse in ethnicity while providing a boost to the mission and vision that God has given the pastor.

A few months before the revitalizer pastor was hired, the church board formally voted to close the longtime community learning center that the church had run for decades. Closing the center was very contentious as it was a longstanding part of the community and, for some, the church's identity. Purveyors of the past thought closing the learning center was akin to closing the church as they were so closely intertwined. The previous years had brought strife, turf wars, and personality conflicts, which caused tension in the shared space between the learning center and church, and for many, they were exhausted. Upon the previous pastor's departure, the district brought in an interim pastor who inherited the turf war. He sought about bringing peace to the warring sides to help the church heal. In reviewing the financials and listening to others, he soon realized that the church board needed to examine the learning center and either make systematic changes or close the center. The board made the tough decision to close the doors effective at the end of that current calendar year, which would be four months after the revitalizer arrived. This caused yet again a mass exodus of members.

The learning center was not the only area of polarization in the church. After a major hurricane struck the area in 2012, the church established a compassionate ministry center as part of its ministry. The leaders enlisted an immigrant to lead the new center as a two-fold mission: to help the immigrant gain his green card, and for the church to help the community. The new director of the center became a polarizing figure in his own right, pitting board members against church members in he said/she said conflicts. The interim pastor did his best to rectify the situation by either lessening the conflicts or moving the director on. When the revitalizer arrived, he was faced with a report from the interim pastor that detailed his concerns. In his trademark fashion, the revitalizer listened and leaned into the problem to better understand what was going on. "I saw firsthand the strengths and weaknesses of the director, but felt he had a heart to serve, and I was willing to help highlight his character strengths overtime," the revitalizer shared about the ensuing years of service together. As the pastor got more acquainted over time with the community, he saw the need for the thrift store lessen, and the need for food increase. He worked with the once-perceived difficult leader to shift the thrift store's programmatic approach to close her doors and increase the distribution of food, as thrift stores in the area had doubled while the food supply had stagnated. This strategic choice to work with the long-term compassionate ministry leader, and evaluate the community needs, helped the revitalizer win over those who might have questioned his leadership. It helped him foster a deeper relationship with the compassionate ministry director to enable them to work together to expand the church's reach into the community for decades to come.

Restoring the Soul

The pastor felt burdened by the call at Seashore Community. His time at the church was challenging but fulfilling in many ways. He knew God was working in the life of the church, he could not only see it, but he sensed it deep in his soul. He began to wonder if God was telling him that his time was drawing to a close. As he walked the church property as he often did, he felt God place in his heart the word "restoration." "It caught me off guard. Why restoration, I asked God?" As he continued to walk, he began to wonder, was God calling him to a season of restoration in his own life? Had he sinned and failed to repent? Did God want to restore the property? His lack of understanding drew the revitalizer into a season of prayer. As he prayed, God began to reveal the plans he had for the pastor. The pastor shared, "Seashore Community was a restless place that would become a resting place for weary souls who are lost but would be found in Christ." After this declaration by God, ministry and mission would collide and focus on restoring lost and broken souls. Where ministries of outreach, notably the learning center and thrift store, had either rebooted or closed, the Lord was leading the pastor to help take his people into the streets to see the invisible that lived around them—translated through a spirit of generosity. Generosity in prayer, giving of resources, and pouring into everyone that church members came in contact with throughout the week.

There had been past years when the church had failed to pay their denominational budgets in full, and through the spirit of restoration, the church committed to repaying their obligation to the district. The church would repay over $15,000 in lost tithing from the church, and with this newfound spirit of restoration, they set out to serve the community they lived in. In a year of struggle for many churches due to a pandemic and downturn in the economy, the church applied for and received a Homeland Security grant that granted them $100,000 to strengthen the church's security measures. The funding provided ample funds to upgrade the church's neglected areas while securing the church from a possible tragic event. "God was showing me that when he said 'restoration,' he was not going to just stop at me, but God was going to restore the full church (people and building)," the pastor said as he shared. Seashore Community has entered a season of restoration and growth because the revitalizer was willing to exhume the past, listen to all sides in the church, and was not afraid of evaluating programs and personnel to expand the kingdom of God outside of the church.

Revitalization Rewards Found in the Work at Seashore Community

1. Be an archaeologist who will examine the past by exhuming where the church has been.

2. Listen to each side, lean into conflict, learn from each conversation, and take lessons from what is learned to move the conversation forward towards healing.

3. Provide space for the "duty bound" to step down in a dignified way, and do not rush to fill their former position.

4. Evaluate all programs and personnel and see how they match up to the vision and then decide on change.

5. Seek God first, obey his will, and follow through.

10

Huntertown

Spiritual Organ Donor

My Way or the Highway

As the pastor packed her items into a box, she smiled as she welcomed me into what had been her office for the last ten and a half years. The Huntertown Church, after sixty-eight years, was ceasing to be a church. In her final act as a dying church, she chose to birth new ministries and gift her property over to a Hispanic church. I was there to hear the details of the birthing and the steps that led to the church's death. The story shared in this chapter could be any church in the preceding chapters with one exception, Huntertown obeyed God to die in order for the kingdom to grow. The warning signs, the waiting, and the relinquishing control over to God should be examined and reexamined as examples for any church that is teetering on the edge of growth or death.

When Huntertown was birthed, she was supported early on by the farmers and families in the rural area. Many of the farms grew tobacco. While the crops yielded income that would be given in tithes, it butted up against the denominational belief system. It kept many of the farmers from entering church membership because of denominational teachings. These hearty farmers while not being allowed to enter full membership due to denominational teachings still gave of their time, talent, and treasure, nonetheless. The farmers would be a significant resource when the church moved to a larger property in 1988. Within a few years, the property would be bordered by middle-class homes with small children and a high potential to expand the ministry to reach these young families. "The church had a great opportunity to reach the community, but she became closed off as pastors transitioned, and members took a firmer hold on things," the last pastor shared. In the sixty-eight years of ministry, Huntertown would have twenty-three pastors, with the final two pastors staying nine and ten-and-a-half years and the average being three years or less. From a member standpoint there was a lack of a perceived commitment on the pastoral family's part which caused trust issues and, ultimately, a possessive streak in the people. "The people did not want to get too close to a pastor or his family because they knew the pastor and his family would just leave," the pastor shared. Over time, individual families began running the church and seemed to take on controlling ownership of many of the ministries. This caused friction among the ruling class of members and newcomers who would come to the church. This would lead to several church splits throughout the decades. With the lack of long-term pastoral leadership, the families divided up the work or, in turn, fought turf battles over control of the church property. "It was not the member's fault; they loved their church and had to step up when the pastor chose not to lead." Each time a new pastor came and established a routine, former members would come back. Before long, the same sentiments that made the members leave before would cause them to leave again. The momentum gained early in the pastor's tenure would be short-lived, which would lead to the departure of the pastoral family and more members leaving, causing the church to spiral into the same cycle every few years for decades.

Mold Breaker

In meeting with the denominational overseer, the evangelist listened to the Huntertown church's plight and how the district did not want to close the legacy work. Huntertown's pastor had just left after nine years of service, and the district was looking for a determined pastor to stick it out and help break the cycles that had been formed over decades. "I only had a desire to lead the church for a month and then move on. I did not feel called to be a pastor but an evangelist," the pastor expressed, reminiscing about that meeting. For fifty-eight years, the church had only male pastors. The thought of having a women pastor was challenging to their image of what members saw a pastor should be. For many in the community having a woman pastor was frowned upon. It was almost threatening to the regular order of things. Yet, God was calling her to take up the mantle and lead Huntertown forward. "Early on, we had success. Partly because people came to see the woman preacher, others came back because that was the cycle they had known, and at other points, we had several visitors." Pastoring was far different from being an evangelist. It became clear rather quickly who ran the church, and it was not her. For the last nine years, a family took over leading the church. It was not because the family wanted to, but because the pastor only showed up on Sunday mornings, and someone had to fill the leadership void. Members divided up the work from paying bills, cleaning, teaching classes, etc. One Sunday morning, the pastor read his entire sermon without ever looking up and closed by saying, "that was what I needed to hear." Later it was discovered by a member that he had found the sermon online and read it word for word. The members did their best to save the legacy church as they felt the pastor did not have time to lead the local church outside of his full-time secular job.

She saw the desperate need to connect with the neighbors around the campus as a next step of sending the message that things had changed at the church. In reaching out on her own, she found out that the church and neighbors had an adversarial relationship. "One of the first things I did was take down the signs that said, 'stay off the grass.'" This one act would allow the neighbors to drive through the church property to reach their property. Taking down the signs was a small gesture on the church's part, but a big sign to the neighbors that things were changing. While the last pastor was able to only come on Sunday mornings, the new pastor immersed herself in helping the community. "I became very involved in the community so people would feel more comfortable, and over time, we saw people start to come." The focused connection helped the church grow. For a church that had weathered many storms, Huntertown seemed to be pressing forward and emerging out of the threat of closure.

Striving for Life

With the influx of new attendees, the church had the momentum to start and expand ministries. The women's ministry was restarted after being dormant for several years over disputes. The men's ministry took off under the leadership of the pastor's husband. The pastor shared, "Community members began attending these two groups, and it was thrilling to see hearts grow closer to God even if they were not weekly members of the church." For ten years the church had a quality Bible quizzing program for children and teens. They won the district championship in three of those years. The church restarted Wednesday night studies but chose the creative route to hold the studies in restaurants in the community, focusing on sharing God's love in tangible ways by praying with the server, the needs of the people around them at other tables, and sharing their faith publicly. Several restaurants shared that they had better business the nights the church held their studies in the establishments. Inside the four walls of the church, the pastor led the people to repent of past sins and give their whole hearts over to Christ. They were tearing down strongholds of the past to prepare for the future. Services turned into powerful God moments where hearts were healed, and the people began to let go of the ownership mentality of the property. The goal of each of these anointed services was for the church to reach lost souls, sometimes those who had been attending for decades. "We did not want just to be a church, but truly to live out the church's mission," the pastor expressed as we stood at the altars inside the empty sanctuary.

Tears, pain, and sorrow were released in this space. The altars for Huntertown were not just pieces of furniture to adorn a sanctuary, but a place where God did a new work.

So how could a church that begun to thrive again, die? Over time some of the positive gains were lost through old disagreements, doctrinal issues as the pastor lead the church to fallow the denominational teachings, and new members upsetting the old order of the church with fresh ideas. Huntertown would enter the most challenging season of her life. "We all knew it was coming to an end, we just wanted to fight to stay open a little longer. The disagreements of the past reared their heads to challenge the new-found unity." The pastor did her best to keep the church focused on prayer, and it was in these prayer times with a few members who would attend that God began to reveal his plans for the Hunter-town church.

Becoming a Donor

Each time the church doors were open, a small but faithful group would attend. "We began to pray that God would do what he wanted to do in the church. We were willing to close if that was God's will." The pastor realized that maybe the church had to grow smaller to grow into the church God was preparing for the next season of her life. God was about to begin answering the pastor's prayers by opening her eyes to see the people group that they were already reaching. Over several summers, the Hunter-town church would host Vacation Bible Schools, and as part of the ending ceremonies, they would host a free community fair giving away household items. The majority of those in attendance would come from the Hispanic community. For an Anglo church, this was the fulfillment of their prayers to reach the community that God wanted them to enter. The pastor and a few key church members began to feel strongly about helping this community. "I knew that summer that this is what God wanted us to do. To give Huntertown away by birthing a Hispanic church to reach the Hispanic community." Even if the pastor had to preach at a future Hispanic service through an interpreter, she would follow God into this new season. Within a month as the pastor sat in a pastoral training on the district, she realized that God was going to open the next door to this burden. A new Hispanic ministry coordinator was announced for the district, and the pastor approached the coordinator about starting a Hispanic work at Huntertown. "It seemed like forever before he got back with me, but God was preparing the way," the pastor shared about the three months of waiting. During this transition time, the Lord laid a burden on a community member's heart. The community member had not connected to the church in any way but had heard Huntertown was a church that would give items away to help those in need. She had decided to give away her full estate as she was liquidating her property. Huntertown set about preparing for their most substantial giveaway and targeted the Hispanic population. The Hispanic coordinator had three other Hispanic churches help with setup, play live music, and interpret for the Anglo church. Through tears, the pastor shared, "It felt like nothing was happening, and I just wanted out of here, and then all of a sudden, God began to move." The coordinator would ask the pastor to come up on stage and share from her heart to those who were gathered, and through an interpreter, she shared the God dream placed on her heart. One of the Hispanic pastors who was invited to help was listening. The Spanish pastor felt God tell her, "This is your new church." With tears streaming down both of their faces, God revelaed that Huntertown would become an organ donor, giving life to a new church.

Within the next few months, both pastors would begin to share the church. During the Hispanic church's opening service, the pastor of Huntertown sat in the last pew, weeping over what God had done as she saw just over forty Hispanic church members praise God in their native tongue. "I had cried many times in that sanctuary over Huntertown dying, but that day I wept at what he (God) had done." The pastor went home that night, smiling in her soul, and knew that God had shown up once more. The next morning, as she lay in bed, she felt the Lord speak deep within her spirit, "You have fought. You have been faithful. You finished your race." She felt released from her call. Over the next few weeks, God would use the pastor's faith to open the next door. A new start church on the district was looking for a home, and Huntertown would open their doors again to provide space for this church.

"It is not about how many bottoms are in the seats when I preach; it is about God moving. If God can move in this new start or a Hispanic church more than mine, then praise God, move Lord," the pastor expressed about that period of expansion. It made sense to the pastor and church board that both churches would take over the Huntertown property, and Huntertown would close. With a formal vote of the board and the district's approval, Huntertown died at the age of sixty-eight. She would leave behind a new Hispanic ministry that would take control of the property, with the new start church sharing space from the Hispanic ministry. The pastor had prayed, "Lord, if I leave, I want to leave with hearts that are focused on you." God had answered her prayer.

There can be dignity in dying, and Huntertown was determined to find that grace as she passed. The final words the pastor shared with me as she finished packing up her office were, "The death of Huntertown gave life to other ministries. It is not a sad thing. People have been saved, sanctified, and called to ministry over the past sixty-eight years. It is not a death but a new beginning. We were winter, and they are spring." The legacy of Huntertown lives on as members dispersed into three other area churches, bringing along a new zest for ministry and community outreach.

Revitalization Rewards Found in the Work at Huntertown

1. Evaluate the effectiveness of ministry and be open to change.

2. A fully surrendered heart can open God opportunities that you could only dream of.

3. God can transform a willing church's heart to reach the lost in the community.

4. Transformation comes to those who seek after the transformer of souls.

5. To die is to gain.

Epilogue

You Are Doing Better Than You Realize

I WAS STRUGGLING IN a small rural church and I wanted to give up. I will never forget the words spoken into my soul by Dr. Phil Fuller, my District Superintendent at the time. Seven simple words that would transform my outlook and encouraged my soul. Dr. Fuller listened patiently as I unloaded my heart which was filled with self-doubt, weariness, and a burden for souls that were not being saved. Seven simple but profound words, in a thirty-minute conversation still impacts me years later, and I pray will impact you. "You are doing better than you realize." Highlight those words. Write them in a notebook that you use daily. Stick them up on your mirror at home. Say it to yourself; I am doing better than I realize. While Dr. Fuller has perhaps forgotten our conversation and possibly even those direct words, his words changed the course of my ministry. Ask yourself, 'what do those words mean to me?' For this struggling pastor, his words altered my life and ministry. In seasons of self-doubt his words spring forth in my mind as a seed long sat dormant in my soul as it burst into a growth spurt and his voice comes to me in a gentle whisper of reassurance. In return I have honored him by sharing the same sequence of words time and time again with other pastors who find themselves in a valley. The work of a revitalization pastor is challenging, and the evil one wants nothing more than to inflict spiritual, personal, and professional pain on the revitalizer in an effort for the pastor to give up and walk away from his calling and/or assignment. The Barna Group says that 1,500 pastors are walking away from ministry monthly. Do not allow the evil one to win. Lean on God, lean on other pastors, and lean into your purpose and calling on your life, because you are doing better than you realize.

Adapting to the Call

Throughout the writing of this book, the world and the church have been tossed upside down due to the Covid-19 pandemic. In my own church we closed our campus for nearly four months and have since reopened with many restrictions. What was once a revitalized work, feels more like a church plant as nearly 50% of the congregation I had preCovid-19 has not come back to in person gatherings. Covid-19 has caused the church to reexamine the way she serves the community of believers. Many pastors have felt the pain I have experienced in the weeks that followed an extended period of closure due to reduced attendance, offerings, and gathering times. If revitalizing was not hard enough, she has now become burdened with trying to figure out the right course to chart in uncertain times. I have had the opportunity to speak with many revitalizers about what should the church do to rebuild amid a pandemic. Some leaders have suggested closing the doors for good and for them to find another profession. I for one do not think that is God's plan for the called leader or the local church. God reminds us that He is the rock, and if we build his church on his Word, the church will make it. Let me encourage you to do four things, *pray, go, return,* and *adapt.* These four things do not have to be just about the pandemic but about the revitalization work.

- *Pray not for a return to normalcy, but a return to being a Christ centered church.*

  How many times have you heard or said yourself; I wish things would return to normal. It is becoming more apparent that things will not return to normal for some time, and maybe that is a good thing. Far too long, the church has operated the same way week after week, with little deviation or room for the Holy Spirit to move. The church is broken, and God is calling her back to centering herself again on him. A time of intentional prayer focuses on what God wants for the church and what He wants for his people. It can be seen as an opportunity not to be lost in the rules and regulations of the local and state governments. While you cannot control what is happening in society, you can control what happens in your soul. Leading your people in intentional prayer times will recenter the church back on Christ and prepare the way for the future.

- *Go smaller to grow back forward.*

  Many local churches are running less than half of what they were running before the pandemic. Instead of seeing less, see God. What an opportunity to become an Acts driven church where the church is not about numbers but about meeting together in small groups to share life. Small groups do not have to be an afterthought in expanding ministry but at the forefront of returning the local church to its biblical mandate and roots. Jesus showed that smaller is better when developing a team of ministry leaders to reach people with the gospel effectively. With twelve men, he helped change the world. Now, imagine with the number of people who have returned, what would happen if they grew smaller to go deeper to come back larger? What a radical transformation would take place in them, in the group, and the larger church.

- *Return to people and not programs.*

  The members have become scattered. Some have disconnected from being a part of the church. Programs had once attracted these members to attend, but today, they are seen as a threat to their health if they gather in large masses. The fear of catching Covid-19, and the time-lapse during the closure have lured once faithful people to stay away. Programs are not what people want; they want to feel connected. For months many have been isolated away from family, friends, and routines. The church has an opportunity to fill the void, by reconnecting with the disconnected. Telephone calls, text messages, social media touchpoints, and old fashion snail mail can make people feel that they are a part of something greater than themselves. Without people coming back to church, there will be no need for programs. Connect with people to share Christ's love, encouragement, and hope for the future.

- *Be adaptable in all ways, always.*

   If you have learned anything as a revitalizer, it should be to be adaptable. By now, you realize that you cannot control what is happening to you or the church, but you can control how you react to the prescribed changes. The rapid amount of change should be seen as an opportunity—and a chance to evaluate everything. Evaluate what are the essentials of worship and what is elevated above worship and discard the latter. Being adaptable is taking away sacred cows and replacing them with God-focused ministry and items that enhance the worshiper's understanding of their faith by allowing them to grow deeper with God. For too many churches, things have become idols and have taken away from the valid reason people come to church. Use this time to change the old ways of hosting church. Do not be constrained by the past but adapt to the present situation and needs of the church.

   Be encouraged, God is still on the throne, and he will work this out for the good of the church if the church is willing to do their part in building the kingdom, and always remember 'you are doing better than you realize.'